I0796877

TO:
FROM:
DATE:

Other Books in the Moments of Grace Series

Moments of Grace for Moms
By Carol Kent and Ellie Kay
Moments of Grace for Grandmas
by Carol Kent and Gracie Malone
Moments of Grace for Teachers
by Carol Kent and Vicki Caruana
Moments of Grace for Women
by Carol Kent and Thelma Wells

To my four remarkable sisters:

Jennie Afman Dimkoff

Paula Afman Brunsting

Bonnie Afman Emmorey

Joy Carlson

Moments of Grace

FOR SISTERS

Stories & Scriptures to Warm Your Heart & Refresh Your Soul

Carol Kent

Visit Christian Art Gifts, Inc., at www.christianartgifts.com.

Moments of Grace for Sisters: Stories & Scriptures to Warm Your Heart & Refresh Your Soul

Previously published by Zondervan as *Kisses of Sunshine for Sisters* © 2005.
Content revised and updated in 2025 by Carol Kent.

Published by Christian Art Gifts, Inc., IL, USA.

First edition 2025.

Designed by Christian Art Gifts, Inc.

Cover and interior images used under license from Shutterstock.com.

In some cases, names have been changed for privacy reasons.

Most Christian Art titles may be purchased at bulk discounts by churches, nonprofits, and corporations. For more information, please email SpecialMarkets@cagifts.com.

ISBN 978-1-63952-897-4

Printed in China.

30 29 28 27 26 25
10 9 8 7 6 5 4 3 2 1

Contents

Introduction

This series of five books—one each for sisters, moms, grandmas, teachers, and women—has lighthearted, uplifting, and often humorous stories meant to bring a sunburst of joy to your life as you remember that God loves you. My own sisters and many friends have joined me in putting these stories together. Our purpose is simply to let God's love so warm and fill you that you become warmth, light, and love to a cold, dark world.

Growing up in a home with five girls and one brother gave me a unique perspective on sisterhood. My sisters and I giggled, shared secrets, borrowed each other's clothes, had an occasional argument, made up, hugged, and carried on with daily life. In the process of growing up, we challenged each other spiritually, celebrated the births of our babies, gathered for family reunions, shared recipes, gave advice on raising strong-willed children, felt one another's hurts, divided the sorrow, multiplied the joy, and cheered when one of our sisters made it to one of life's occasional milestones.

All of my sisters are masterful storytellers. In fact, we've told each other that we have an amazing ability to make a good story *better* than what actually happened. When we get together, we often tell stories of recent experiences and then brainstorm to find the hidden life lesson in the incident. According to a quote widely attributed to Chris

Montaigne, "A sister smiles when one tells one's stories, for she knows where the decoration has been added." We hope you enjoy reading these stories as much as we enjoyed writing them.

If you have a biological sister, a sister-in-law, an adopted sister, a sister-of-the-heart, or a sister-in-the-Lord, this book is for you. I hope these stories will make you laugh out loud, encourage you to be a more creative sister, motivate you to make a difference in your world, and inspire you to deepen your faith walk.

This is a book you can read before bedtime, in the car, at the beach, or in the bathroom. Each story is a short vignette that might tickle your funny bone or move you to dry a tear. I challenge you to take a break in your busy day, pour a cup of tea or coffee (your choice), put your feet up, and read a chapter. You'll be glad you did.

Doin' the Pinkie Swing

– Dawn Baker –

> The bond between sisters is unique, stretching and bending through periods of closeness and distance, but almost never breaking.
>
> Carol Saline, from *Sisters*

My mother was only twenty-four years old when she died in an automobile accident, leaving three small children. My little brother was six months old, I was a year and a half, and my big sister was almost three. Dona and I are only seventeen months apart, and during our growing-up years we always shared a bedroom.

Many nights we went to bed afraid and lonely, and we were somewhat confused about life. Dona wasn't sheepish about her nighttime fears; I always tried to hide mine. Our bedroom was small, and we had twin beds that were always next to each other, separated only by the walking distance between them. Frequently, well after we should have been asleep, Dona would whisper to me, "Are you awake?" Often I pretended I hadn't heard her. If I answered, she would sometimes ask if she could climb into bed with me for a while. More often she just kept asking in a louder and more intense whisper, "Are you awake?" until I finally answered, or until she did wake me up!

My sister always wanted to talk, but after I became tired, she would settle for a slim amount of physical contact. She would whisper "pinkies" to me, and I knew what that meant. We would reach across the narrow space between our beds, both lying on our tummies, hook our pinkie fingers together, and swing them to comfort each other. The touch of a sister's hand consoled both of us. Finally we would fall asleep peacefully.

I never realized how much our "pinkie swing" meant to me until she went away to college a year and a half ahead of me. Suddenly I was gripped with fear, finding myself in a bedroom at night all alone for the first time. I started pinning Scripture to my window shade, then pulling it down to eye level and reading it over and over again until sleep overtook me. "Thou wilt keep him in perfect peace, whose mind is stayed on thee" (Isaiah 26:3 KJV). "In peace I will lie down and sleep, for you alone, LORD, make me dwell in safety" (Psalm 4:8). These words brought a calm and peace to my heart.

Dona and I are grown women now, and both of us know that Scripture is the best antidote to fear. As adults, Dona and I occasionally have a chance to hang out together. We still face fearful situations. With a smile, one of us will call out "pinkie swing," and we instantly know the comfort and courage that comes from a supportive sister. God gave two little girls reassurance through "the nights of life." And He's still doing that today.

"So do not fear, for I am with you;
do not be dismayed, for I am your God.
I will strengthen you and help you;
I will uphold you with my righteous right hand."

ISAIAH 41:10

Two Cooks and a Skillet of Noodles

– Bonnie Afman Emmorey –

It is bad to suppress your laughter.
It goes back down and spreads to your hips.

Fred Allen

Being the fourth daughter born in the Afman household had one big advantage. I never had to learn how to cook. If Mother was gone, one of my older sisters took over the meal preparation.

After our sisters Carol and Jennie left for college, Paula and I became the oldest of four children still living at home. Our mother soon realized there was a problem. Paula is just eighteen months older than I am, and she hadn't learned how to cook either. I was a junior in high school, and Paula was a freshman in college. By this time Mother didn't have much hope that a crash course in home economics would help us.

It was the seventies—long before there was a microwave oven in every kitchen. Mother kept a stash of pot pies in the freezer for us. If we came home and found ourselves on our own, we would just pop a pie in the oven and we had dinner.

One summer day Paula and I arrived home after working all day, and no one else was there. No problem. I flipped on the switch to preheat the oven and left the room to change my clothes. Paula and I were back in the kitchen about a half hour later, ready to put in the pot pies—but we discovered a problem. Mom had left two pounds of ground beef in the oven to thaw.

We had a dilemma! The meat was already half-cooked, and we knew Mother wouldn't be happy if it was wasted, so we decided to make something out of it. We scrounged through the cupboards and found a box of Hamburger Helper. Surely this box would solve our problem.

Paula got out the electric skillet and finished cooking the meat while I prepared to mix in the remaining ingredients. I was a little concerned because the mix called for one pound of meat and we had two, but Paula assured me that we could make it work.

Once everything was in the pan, we weren't too sure. Our concoction didn't look very appetizing. The box said we were making goulash, but there was way too much meat. We knew we'd have to add more ingredients. Paula suggested it needed more color, so she added a whole quart of Mother's canned tomatoes. I thought it needed more noodles to balance out all the tomatoes, so I found a box of elbow macaroni and dumped that into the mixture. We replaced the lid and prayed for a miracle.

A few minutes later, something odd happened. Our makeshift dinner was oozing out from under the lid and running down the side of the pan. When Paula lifted the cover, our creation poured out. The original mixture had *doubled* in size and was continuing to grow. The noodles were expanding—getting bigger and bigger! Our concoction was running off the stove and down onto the floor. We were in trouble—and we knew it.

At that moment Mother and Dad came in the door. Paula and I were trying not to fall on the slippery noodles now spread across the floor and trying to keep some of our dinner in the pan. But it kept coming and coming. We soon realized our situation was out of control. Even Mother recognized the humor of the moment, and we stood there in the middle of those slimy noodles and laughed out loud. Here we were—two grown women—and we couldn't even make Hamburger Helper!

It soon occurred to us that we hadn't read the directions. Who knew that noodles had to be *cooked* before they were added to the other ingredients? Even Mother couldn't save our creation. It was beyond hope! We tried giving it to the dog, but even she turned her nose up at it. After cleaning up the awful mess, our whole family ate pot pies.

Paula and I are both grown now, and we *did* eventually learn how to cook. However, we still break into a sweat when we see a box of Hamburger Helper. And we often find ourselves laughing uncontrollably when we watch noodles expand in hot water. Together we discovered that *following directions* is an important part of life.

Those who listen to instruction will prosper;
Those who trust the Lord will be joyful.

PROVERBS 16:20 NLT

I Got Your Back

– Dr. Nancy Meyer –

A sister is a little bit of childhood that can never be lost.

Marion C. Garretty

Until my identical twin sister, Stephanie, and I were in the fifth grade, our mom always dressed us in matching outfits. We looked exactly alike at that time (and we still do, apart from our hairstyles); even our voices sounded the same. The only difference between us was caused by an injury I got during the emergency C-section when I was born.

My parents didn't know they were having twins until we were born, and they couldn't tell us apart until we were six months old and our personalities started coming out. They would lift our little gowns, looking for my tiny scar, to keep track of which of us was fed, which needed to be changed, and which was ready for a nap.

One weekend our mom took us with her on a shopping trip. She was looking for an outfit for a special occasion, and we got to tag along—great fun for two six-year-olds. Window displays of fancy dresses lured us into this little boutique that smelled heavenly from women's perfumes.

Everything sparkled from the sunlight cascading through large glass windows, especially the gorgeous sequin dresses. It seemed like a place designed for royalty.

A step divided the back of the store from the front. The back area was slightly elevated, and Stephanie and I thought it was great fun to have that step in the middle of the store. While our mom tried on clothes, my sister and I walked back and forth, doing laps up and down the step. On our circular route around the store, we zigzagged through clothes racks and said *hi* to other patrons. We were well-behaved but very energetic.

One customer who enjoyed watching us play offered me a stick of gum but not Stephanie. I immediately asked, "Can I have one more?"

The woman looked confused at my seeming greed. "Why?" she asked.

I politely responded, "For my sister."

She looked even more confused. "I don't see your sister, sweetie."

Mustering my most convincing dose of six-year-old courage, I explained that I needed another piece of gum for my identical twin sister, who was with me in the store. But she wasn't buying my explanation. I called Stephanie over so the woman could see us together.

The woman's mouth dropped open in astonishment when I presented my sister to her. I was grinning from ear to ear. I was proud of Stephanie, and I was proud of being a twin. I didn't want anything she didn't have, so it was only fair my sister receive a piece of gum too.

After staring at us for a moment, the lady eventually understood this. "I didn't realize there were two of you. You look exactly alike," she said, laughing. "I wondered how you went back and forth so quickly." She handed us another piece of gum. "I can't tell you apart. I thought you were the same person."

This scenario is just like life. We don't always see what's happening. Stephanie didn't know I had gotten a piece of gum without her, but she knew she could count on me to have her back. In the same way, we can always count on God to be there with something good in store for us, even when we can't see it. He always looks out for us. He brings sisters into our lives to be a blessing to us and so that we can be a blessing to them.

A true sister is one who looks out for you, speaks up for you, and supports you. And our sisters, whether blood relatives or sisters in Christ, are here to have our backs through all life's ups and downs.

Therefore encourage one another
and build one another up, just as you are doing.

1 THESSALONIANS 5:11 ESV

The Throne Room

– Carol Kent –

Sisters and friends are God's life preservers.

Anonymous

My best childhood memories are from the year we moved into the big old farmhouse at the end of Foreman Road. The main road dead-ended at the edge of our property line, and very few people ventured down this country lane without an invitation. It would have been a lonely time in my life, except for one key fact—I already had three sisters (one more would be born later, but we didn't know about her yet). And nobody could feel alone for long with that many girls in the house.

The farmhouse had a big old space heater in the living room, and that room was connected to the kitchen, the music room, the master bedroom, the bathroom, and the steps that led to the sisters' quarters upstairs. The house was the commanding cornerstone for thirty-five acres of farmland, but it had one main flaw. In spite of numerous bedrooms, there was only *one* bathroom in that gigantic old house. That room defied the norm for the period in which it was built because it was a *big* bathroom, complete with an old-fashioned shower. All of my sisters enjoyed taking their turn standing in the robust stream of water that cascaded from the antiquated showerhead.

Near the shower was the commode—and with so many people in our family, it was often in use. Our mother referred to this popular appliance as "the throne," and often one would hear a voice outside the door saying, "Is anybody sitting on the throne now? I need to get in there!" Very quickly this room was dubbed "The Throne Room."

The Throne Room also contained the best mirror in the house for squeezing pimples and putting on makeup, so it was not uncommon to have one sister in the shower, one at the mirror, another with her head propped on a floor pillow in front of the hamper, and another sitting on the "throne," with or without the lid down. Some of my most memorable talks with my sisters took place in this wonderful, confined space, where all pretense was gone and honest repartee, mindless bantering, and humorous jousting took place on a regular basis. We discussed coming-of-age, boys, church, clothes, and beauty tips. Often, the wrinkled skin on the sister who did her talking through the shower curtain served as a reminder that we had all been in the room too long.

My sisters are grown now, but some things in life don't change much. Last weekend my husband and I were visiting our granddaughters in Florida. It was the night before we were to leave to catch an early plane home. While in the bathroom removing my makeup, I soon realized I wasn't alone. Seven-year-old Hannah had slipped into the empty bathtub fully clothed and settled in for some conversation. Chelsea, age ten, positioned herself near the towel rack. Their mama soon claimed the throne (lid down), and our conversation quickly became animated.

Glancing over at Hannah, I noticed numerous unclothed Barbie dolls in the wire rack attached to the bathtub. With a chuckle I said to the girls, "What's the deal with all of these naked dolls in the tub?"

Hannah immediately picked up one of the dolls. "This is Olympic Barbie and she's teaching the rest of the girls how to swim, but we didn't want to get their clothes wet, so we took them off." My granddaughter hit a button on the back of the doll and sure enough, Olympic Barbie began to do the breaststroke. "She even has a gold medal," Hannah cheerfully added. We all laughed as they demonstrated the swimming lessons.

My eyes soon landed on the only male doll in the group. Poor Ken was missing both his legs. Evidently Olympic Barbie had worn the guy out with her advanced swimming techniques. The girls giggled as their mommy picked up the physically impaired Ken and used her own fingers to make new appendages for him. Quite unexpectedly he was leaping and running and even looked somewhat normal. Laughter again filled the room.

Suddenly there was a moment of silence and Hannah piped up with, "Grammy, why can't you stay longer? Why do you have to leave us tomorrow? We don't want you to go yet."

A warm, familiar emotion engulfed me as I looked around that room at two little sisters, their mom, and me—Grammy Carol. I realized that girls seem to talk best in the confined quarters of "the throne room." It felt good. It felt right.

Love one another deeply, from the heart.

1 PETER 1:22

Sister Squad to the Rescue

– Pam Cronk –

There is a special bond and a unique strength shared between sisters.

Anonymous

It was a cloudless, sunny morning. The phone rang and following my cheery greeting, I heard my brother-in-law say, "Hi. This is Mike. Our house burned down this morning." He spoke stoically. After telling us that nobody was hurt, he explained some of the details. Then he said, "Here, I'll let you talk to your sister."

An emotional conversation ensued. Our Mom joined the conversation, and we learned that although the house was still standing, the contents were all burned, melted, or charred. Stunned and in tears, Mom and I told Lois that we would pray, and we would let the rest of the family know.

As I hung up, one of Lois's comments lingered in my mind: "We're watching the firemen try to save some of our memories, but nothing really matters except our family's safety and our relationship with the Lord. We know God is in control and has a reason for this."

I called my other two sisters. The following day we worked out the details of jobs and family that would free us to travel from our home in Michigan to Wisconsin to comfort and help our sister and her family during this crisis. We were not fully aware of what we would face. So, equipped with industrial-strength dust-and-particle masks, gloves, work clothes, a laptop, and as much cheer as we could muster, we prayerfully left on our four-hundred-mile road trip.

We spent our travel time reminiscing about many "sister weekends," knowing that what lay ahead would be a totally different kind of reunion. Still, we hoped to bring in some of the heartwarming fun and craziness we always experienced when we had sister-time together. The three of us created makeshift badges to wear that would serve as smile-makers when we arrived in Wausau for the big clean-up operation. They read: "SEARCH, SNIFF, SCRATCH, SWEEP ... SISTER SQUAD TO THE RESCUE!"

As we drove up to their home, we saw our sister and brother-in-law dressed in borrowed clothes, working in the garage with Mike's sister. Lois squealed as she came to greet us. We got out and charged up the driveway with our masks, gloves, and badges on. Our appearance did bring laughter, along with tears. We enjoyed a group hug and then quickly got to work.

Our job was to sort through items that could be restored and categorize them on inventory sheets. It was over 95 degrees outside and much hotter in the charred, stench-filled shell that had been our sister's lovely home. As we worked, we made jokes when we found items all of us remembered. Periodically Lois said, "I am so glad to have my sisters here with me. You have come to my rescue!"

As that first exhausting day came to a close, we decided Lois should stay with us at the hotel. She arrived carrying a borrowed child-sized, floral suitcase, and we all burst into laughter. "I'm going to Grandma's!" Lois exclaimed, chuckling. We spent the rest of the evening in the pool getting some needed hydrotherapy.

The rest of the week, us four wiped-out sisters reminisced, cried, prayed, inventoried household goods, wiped soot off ourselves, watched dumpsters being packed and hauled away, and investigated new possibilities for furniture and other necessary items. We talked on the phone with out-of-town family members, snuggled, ate meals with gracious friends and neighbors, enjoyed chocolate from our traditional "Sisters' Chocolate Smorgasbord," completed a hard copy of the insurance inventory, and bonded more closely than ever before.

We realized, along with Mike and Lois, that material things aren't the important things in life. It's the loving relationships God has given us with Himself and with our family. Our Sister Rescue Squad was a reminder that in good times and bad times sisters need each other.

And we know that in
all things God works for the
good of those who love him,
who have been called
according to his purpose.

ROMANS 8:28

The Graduation Dress

– Jennie Afman Dimkoff –

In the cookies of life, sisters are the chocolate chips.

Anonymous

"Hey Jen, are you home?" my sister Paula called as she came in my back door, loaded with a big, black garbage bag.

"Hi, sis!" I laughed as she was approaching. "What's in the bag?"

"You take this," she said, transferring the heavy bag to me. "I've also got a goodie box I think you may be able to use that's still in my car."

I was curious, so I plopped the big bag on the floor and peeked inside. I found lovely draperies and even blackout curtains ideal for a bedroom. I looked up to see Paula hefting a good-sized box through the entryway. I pointed to the bag on the floor. "These are lovely. Why are you getting rid of them?"

"I've decided to put up wooden blinds in all the windows of our lake house, so all these have gotta go. This box is full of long, sheer, white panels. I've washed them, so they're clean and like new. Do you have a use for them?"

"As a matter of fact, I do," I said, "and your timing is perfect! I'm staging our rental house on Merchant Street, and the last tenant took all the curtains. I was going out to buy new ones today."

Paula laughed. "Well, since I saved you shopping time and money, do you have time to grab a salad at The Lunch Pail downtown? After we eat, I'll help you hang the curtains! I don't have all afternoon free, but I'd love to spend some time with you."

Over lunch Paula reminisced with a sweet, yet somewhat mischievous smile. "Do you remember my high school graduation dress?"

I nodded, smiling. She was bringing up ancient history.

"It was soft, sheer-white, with matching lace. You made it for me, and I felt like an absolute princess. You even included a pearl necklace. Mom and Dad couldn't afford a new dress, and you and Graydon were poverty-stricken newlyweds. It wasn't until long after graduation that you told me you made that gorgeous dress out of thrift-store lace curtains." With a huge grin she added, "Isn't it only right that I should bring you my used curtains after all these years?"

We burst into laughter and headed to the rental house. Paula's lovely draperies made the vacant rental look more like a tasteful home. She had to leave before we were finished, and as I sat on the floor, fingering the sheer, white panels in the open box, my mind went back to our earlier conversation.

Paula had graduated from a private high school where graduation didn't mean simply wearing a dark cap and gown. A graduation "dress" was expected. Dad was the pastor of a small church, and he and Mom had six children. There was no money in the budget for a fancy dress. My husband was in law school, I was an undergrad, and our budget was so tight there was nothing to spare. But while visiting a local thrift shop, I had an idea. I would *make* her dress. I found the most beautiful soft, sheer, white curtains with lace trim for almost nothing! Upon checking out, I spotted a sweet pearl necklace in the case for just one dollar. I was sure it would look lovely with the dress.

Paula felt like a princess on graduation day, and she had no idea she was wearing curtains.

Sitting on the floor next to the open box, I smiled at the memories. "Lord," I began to pray, "thank you for my sweet sister, Paula. Thank you for providing a princess dress for her graduation so many years ago and for making it possible for me to be part of that wonderful surprise. Thank you for your timing today, for my sister's generosity, and for the beautiful drapes and curtains—

Just then my cell phone rang. It was Paula. "Hey Jen," she said, "I forgot to tell you that a few years ago I took that pearl necklace you gave me for graduation to a jeweler. It was appraised at two hundred dollars! Thanks again! Love you, sis!

I will sing for joy in GOD,
explode in praise from deep in my soul!
He dressed me up in a suit of salvation,
he outfitted me in a robe of righteousness.

ISAIAH 61:10 MSG

Blessed Assurance in the Hayloft

– Carol Kent –

There is some unwritten rule between sisters that you are there for each other, no matter what the situation.

Lori Shankle

If walls could talk, the farmhouse and barn at the end of Foreman Road could fill a book. The house sat high on a hill, and the yard sloped gently down to a picturesque rippling creek that flowed across many of the farm's thirty-five acres. On the other side of the house stood a tall weeping willow tree, gracing the yard with fairy-tale charm. Just beyond the big circle driveway stood the barn. Dad wasn't a farmer, but he rented space in that aging structure to neighbors, who filled the lofts with bales of hay.

That hayloft provided endless hours of fun for me and my sisters. Our adventuresome cousin Ronnie would stack the bales of hay to create a maze of hidden passageways where we could hide without being discovered. Whenever other children visited, we would busy ourselves for hours and never tire of the fun that could be found in that old, dilapidated barn.

I often sought the solitude of the barn when life got hectic, and the hayloft was a favorite place for me to read. Just enough sunshine came through the slats that I could get some very good light high in the loft area. It became my place of solitude for spending time alone with God.

One day as I was having my quiet time in the hayloft, I heard footsteps. My sister Jennie had found my favorite place. The look on her face told me something was wrong. Although four years separated us in age, there was a tender closeness in our relationship. Jennie had rheumatic fever that required long rest periods, and she often grew weary of the time she had to spend in bed.

"What's wrong, Jennie?"

My little sister paused a moment and then blurted out her secret. "Carol, one afternoon when I was five years old, I didn't want to go back to bed. I knew Mama would listen to me for a long time if I talked about the Lord, and that night I asked her about what it meant to be a real Christian. She took lots of time and told me that Jesus paid the price for my sins when He died on the cross and that He rose from the dead. She asked me if I wanted to be born into God's family and I told her I did. I asked lots more questions, and finally Mama prayed with me and I asked Jesus to come into my heart."

Jennie was crying by this time. I tried to be encouraging.

"That's a good thing, Jen. You became a Christian that day. Why are you crying?"

With agonizing sobs, my almost-eight-year-old sister confessed, "The afternoon I prayed with Mama, I didn't want to go to back to bed, and I think I'm probably not really a Christian, and I'm probably going to hell because I think I just prayed that prayer with her so I could stay up later."

Guilt is a cruel companion, and my tenderhearted sister had finally revealed her deepest fear. Seeing me in the hay-loft reading my Bible had triggered her confession.

At twelve years of age, I felt an enormous responsibility and a joy-filled opportunity as I slipped an arm around my sister. "Jennie, if you're not positive that you're a Christian, let's pray right now. You can pray that prayer again, and if you didn't really mean it the first time, you can know *for sure* that you've been born into God's family today."

That afternoon two sisters got down on their knees side by side next to a bale of hay, and Jennie sweetly confessed her sin to God and asked Jesus to be her Savior. As we stood up, her face was beaming, the assurance of her faith replacing a guilty conscience.

Jennie had become a "for real" Christian.

For the wages of sin is death, but the gift of God is eternal life in Christ Jesus our Lord.

ROMANS 6:23

My Hair-Brained Extreme Makeover

– Brenda Fassett –

Big sisters are the crab grass in the lawn of life.

Charles M. Schultz

The summer I turned eight started out normal enough. My sister Sheila, age seven, and I had finished our school year at the end of May. We were giddy with the prospect of long days of play and high adventure. The fact that I had an early June birthday was the icing on the cake. Cake indeed! And ice cream! And presents! Within days, my aunt Charlotte arrived with a small swimming pool in tow. Life didn't get any better than this.

But after a few days of swimming and splashing, we got an itch to do other things—like playing with our "old, faithful" toys. Sheila and I pulled out our tried-and-true Barbie and Midge dolls. We each had one doll. Midge was my favorite. She had beautiful, long auburn hair styled in a permanent pageboy. Sheila had a classic blonde pony-tailed Barbie.

Then I came up with a brilliant idea, sort of an *extreme* makeover! I was so excited I could barely speak. "Sheil," I squealed, "let's make Barbie wigs!"

"Barbie wigs? What do you mean?" she asked.

"Let's make wigs for our Barbies so they can have new hairdos. It'll be great!"

"How do you make Barbie wigs, Brenny?"

"It's easy. You take some hair and put it on the doll's head, okay?" I was about to burst with excitement!

"Where do we get the hair from, Bren?"

"Well, I guess we'll have to use yours," I said.

Sheila's eyes flew open, and her face turned white. "*My* hair? Why *my* hair? Why not *your* hair?"

"Well, we *can* use my hair, but do you know how to cut hair for wigs? I've got a pretty good idea of how to do it. Do *you*?"

Her shoulders slumped. She knew my advanced age and superior skills had her beat. "How much hair?" she asked, stroking her shoulder-length hair.

"Not much."

"Mom will know," she said matter-of-factly.

"I'll just take a little from the back. She won't notice."

"You really, *really* know how to make Barbie wigs, Brenny?"

"Yes," I said, lying unashamedly.

I got the scissors and went to work. I cut. And I cut. And I cut some more.

Before long there was *a lot* of hair on the floor. It wasn't hanging in nice straight sections like Sheila's haircut anymore. It was just a pile of hair. A big, messy mishmash pile of hair. A no-rhyme-or-reason pile of hair.

Then I looked at Sheila's head. I was aghast! Most of the hair from the back of her head was gone! How had I cut it so short? How had I cut so *much*? Suddenly an overwhelming truth surged through my brain—this was a really, really, really bad idea!

Sheila turned around and saw all her hair on the floor. With the hopeful eyes of a trusting little sister, she held up a fistful. "So how do we make it into wigs, Brenny?"

That moment is forever emblazed in my mind. I had let my sister down before, but this was the first time I had blown it in such a big way. How would I answer her?

"I don't know," I admitted.

"What do you mean you don't know? You said you knew how!"

"I thought I did."

"You *said* you did!"

"I thought I did."

Sheila felt the back of her head and started to cry. I didn't have enough sense to cry. But I had a plan. I convinced my sister that if she stayed in the swimming pool all day, Mom wouldn't notice her hair because it would be wet. Sheila ran for the pool, where she submerged her head and stayed wet for the remainder of the afternoon.

At suppertime, a waterlogged Sheila was ordered out of the pool. Mom saw her hair. We confessed to the crime and were given our sentence. Sheila would have to get a very short haircut to fix the mess I had made, and I, as the originator of the idea, would receive the same haircut.

I meekly asked Sheila to forgive me for talking her into such a bad idea. She put her arm around me and said, "It's okay, Brenny. It will be fun to have the same haircut this summer." And so it was that the two oldest sisters both had fashionable "pixies" for the entire summer.

This wasn't the last wild idea I dreamed up, but over time I learned the art of looking before leaping. I also learned that if you're going to plan a *hair-brained* scheme, there's no better person to bring along for the ride than your sister.

Be kind and compassionate
to one another, forgiving each other,
just as in Christ God forgave you.

EPHESIANS 4:32

A Tribute to "Foo Foo"

– Carol Kent –

To get the full value of joy, you must have someone to divide it with.

Mark Twain

My sister Paula Sue came out of the womb with big, bright eyes; fine, silky hair; a perfect complexion; pink, tulip-shaped lips; and an ability to bring sunshine into any situation. As the baby became an adolescent and puberty evolved her into a grown woman, heads turned when she entered a room. When Paula grew up, her smile could make a ship full of sailors jump overboard in hopes of being rescued by this beauty.

You might think the above description would bring envy to a family with five girls, but this wasn't the case. Certain people are born to bring optimism, hope, and joy to this world, and Paula is one of those people. Our pet name for Paula is "Foo Foo," which to her sisters means "This girl was born for celebration and spontaneity!"

A short while ago, I wrote a list of the things I appreciate most about her.

To My Pretty Foo Foo,

- You always make me feel loved.
- When I call, you don't act like I've interrupted your day and you have "things to do" that are more important than my problems.
- You dress in a funky, delightfully flamboyant way that makes heads turn when you enter a room.
- You have big hair, glamorous makeup, sparkling jewelry, high energy, and exciting ideas for outrageous getaways.
- You make everyone in the room feel important.
- You are never embarrassed to do wacky things.
- You are still young enough at heart to play dress-up.
- You have become "Auntie Foo Foo" to your nieces and nephews, and they know when you arrive, fun and celebration are walking into the room too.
- You would give your last dime to help a sister in need.
- You have demonstrated how to survive the loss of a marriage, the devastation of betrayal, and the death of a dream—and you have successfully climbed out of the "stuff" of life to show me how to smile again, even when life is hard.

Biologically speaking, we can't pick our sisters. But when you get a good one, you know it. My pretty Foo Foo was custom designed by God to be in my family because He knew how much I would need the sunshine of her smile.

A good woman is hard to find, and worth far more than diamonds. Her clothes are well-made and elegant, and she always faces tomorrow with a smile. When she speaks she has something worthwhile to say, and she always says it kindly.

PROVERBS 31:10, 25–26 MSG

What Would *You* Like, Sis?

– Lucinda Secrest McDowell –

The best things in life aren't things.

Anonymous

"If y'all don't want the silver tea service, I'd love to have it," I said to my two sisters as we surveyed our parents' vast living and dining rooms.

"No problem, Cindy. I could really use the bronze fireplace fixtures," Susan said.

"That's great because I'd love to give Catharine this dining room set for her little family, if y'all agree," Cathy pointed out.

And so it went—three adult sisters from three different parts of the country meeting to divide our parents' home furnishings. A month earlier Mama and Daddy had moved to a small apartment in a nearby retirement community. They had lovingly furnished it with their favorite things. But it couldn't hold everything collected during fifty-five years of marriage, so they invited us to divide up the rest for ourselves and for our children.

What a daunting task! We had all heard horror stories of

siblings fighting over who got what, but here we were making decisions amicably. *Sisters* were obviously greater than *stuff*! Whenever two or more of us wanted the same thing, we simply drew straws or rotated the picking process.

I'm not saying it wasn't hard. We had to make quick decisions, and the magnitude of the task threatened to overwhelm us. But even in the emotional stress of dismantling our family home, we each remembered what our parents had taught us well—*people are more important than things*.

As we sorted through the house, we were each drawn to certain objects because of a sentimental attachment or a fond memory associated with them. Not once did anyone say, "How much is this worth?" These items were precious to us because they were an extension of our parents and their legacy of love.

It took us a full week, and though we got tired and even frustrated, we never argued over one single thing. In fact, it drew us even closer together as sisters since we reminisced the whole time. I consider this to be an extraordinary tribute to our parents' raising us with godly priorities.

Today our respective homes in Connecticut, Oklahoma, and Georgia are each made cozier by the objects we chose and will pass down to our children. And Mama and Daddy can enjoy them whenever they visit.

"Do not lay up for yourselves treasures on earth, where moth and rust destroy and where thieves break in and steal, but lay up for yourselves treasures in heaven, where neither moth nor rust destroys and where thieves do not break in and steal. For where your treasure is, there your heart will be also."

MATTHEW 6:19–21 ESV

Bubbles and Troubles

– Bonnie Afman Emmorey –

Double, double toil and trouble;
Fire burn and caldron bubble.

Shakespeare, from *Macbeth*

On Saturday in the Afman household there were two things we could count on. First, we would spend the day cleaning. Second, we would be in line for the bathtub scrub. In case you're wondering, this wasn't the only day we bathed, but on Saturday nights it was mandatory. Come Sunday morning, there would be a row of shiny-clean faces in the Afman pew at church. (With six children in our family, we took up a whole pew.)

Our Dutch heritage was most evident on those Saturdays. As the old saying goes, "Cleanliness is next to godliness," and at our home that meant house *and body*! Since my sister Paula was the closest in age to me, we often bathed together in those early years. We had such fun, splashing and laughing in that oversized, old-fashioned tub.

At the time of "the bubble incident," Paula was seven years old and I was six. Our turn for the bathtub came and, with it, a wonderfully creative idea was born. We decided to take our mother's dish soap, add it to our bathwater, and make a wonderful, foamy bathing extravaganza. Our idea worked to perfection. We poured almost the whole bottle of soap into the water, jumped in, and stood side by side facing the long slope of that big, comfortable, old bathtub. We leaned forward, placed our hands at the top of the slope to give us balance, and started to run in place. Using our unlimited supply of youthful energy, we churned and agitated the water, and the soapy bubbles started to billow and foam.

Before long we had a beautiful mass of bubbles towering over the top edge of that tub. We laughed jubilantly and played to our hearts' content. Paula and I created high, bouffant hairstyles. We gave ourselves voluptuous, womanly bubble figures. We played in the tub of bubbles until our fingers and toes were as shriveled as prunes.

Unfortunately, we had not thought ahead. We let out all the water and, to our amazement, the bubbles stayed behind. A fitting caption would have been "*Bubble, bubble,* toil and trouble"! We had just as many bubbles *without* the water. In fact, in our young minds it seemed they were still *growing*. We began to panic. Our mother was not going to be happy that we had wasted most of her dish soap; we pictured major trouble in our immediate future.

We *had* to get rid of those bubbles. Paula and I had created them with such delight and enjoyment. We needed to get rid of them with the same intensity. We tried flushing them by adding water. That was a mistake! It only created more bubbles and more trouble. We tried clapping them. Too slow. We knew we'd be working on this mission way past our bedtime—and we'd be caught. But when you put two Afman girls together, they can solve almost anything.

Paula and I moved into action. We discovered that it was possible to crush and dissolve the bubbles by taking our washcloths and smothering them. It was a long, laborious job. We were exhausted from our hard work. But we continued until every bubble was gone. Down the drain. Crushed into oblivion. Our troubles were over! We got away with it! Our mother was not going to find out after all.

More than forty years have since passed, yet the memory is still vivid. This past Christmas, Paula, Mother, and I were vacationing in Florida and the bubble incident was revisited. With much laughter, Paula and I *finally* admitted to Mother what we had done. Mother laughed right along with us, assuring us that she never knew about the "bubble extravaganza," and she never missed the soap.

Even though Paula and I now live almost a continent apart, we still share our bubbles and troubles regularly. When we're together, laughter bubbles out of us, and our troubles seem to float away. When we're apart, cell phones and the internet keep us connected. Participating in ongoing sister escapades gives us great joy. We have bubbled with trouble in the past and I'm sure we will bubble with trouble in the future, but I have every confidence that, together, we will work hard to dissolve our disasters and multiply our joys. Life's problems are always easier to handle with a sister at your side.

Friends love through all kinds of weather,
and families stick together in all kinds of trouble.

PROVERBS 17:17 MSG

A Picture Is Worth a Thousand Words

– Barbara Bond-Howard –

You don't make a photograph just with a camera. You bring to the act of photography all the pictures you have seen, the books you have read, the music you have heard, the people you have loved.

Ansel Adams

If you were alive on September 11, 2001, you probably remember what you were doing. But do you remember September 10, 2001? I remember it well. My sister, Jeanie, had flown from Green Bay, Wisconsin, back to my home in Washington State after our dad died. We claimed his ashes a few days earlier, and we were spending time together.

On September 10, we decided to have a "sisters picture" taken. We went shopping to find matching shirts to go with our already matching Venetian crosses. But we had a problem. Everything that looked good on her didn't look good on me. The clothes I liked, she didn't. Jeanie wanted to keep shopping for clothes, and I just wanted to go to a bookstore and bury myself in some good reading.

"Barbie," she said, using my childhood name, "this is so much fun!" I brushed it off. It *wasn't* fun. Dad had died, his remains were in my car, and I was supposed to find a shirt that was flattering, all so that we could have our (*gasp*) picture taken?

My usually optimistic nature was not kicking in. I was sad. I didn't want a new shirt. I didn't want to be in a mall. And I certainly didn't want my picture taken. I wanted my dad back. We finally agreed on matching shirts, and we got our picture taken. This was long before digital pictures were being taken on cell phones, so while the photos were being processed, we had lunch together, knowing that our "sister time" was quickly coming to a close. When the pictures were ready, we returned to my home so she could pack.

Today our mom has this picture proudly framed in her study. Jeanie has her copy prominently placed in her family room. My duplicate picture is stuffed in a desk drawer because I don't want to be reminded of how sad I felt that day. Jeanie looks pretty good in the photo, and I look—well, I look *depressed*.

My sister had been scheduled to fly home the next day, but we woke up to the tragedy of the World Trade Center disaster and the horrifying news of the other terrorist attacks. We soon learned Jeanie wouldn't be taking any flights that day. We were devastated by the events of September 11 and still mourning our father's death. If my September

10 photo looked depressing, then I am glad there were no photos taken of me on September 11.

It was four days before Jeanie was able to leave for her home via train. During our unexpected time together, we drove up to Mount Baker Lake in the Cascade Mountains and took a ferry ride through Puget Sound. All the while we continued sharing memories of Dad and his influence on our lives. Then I suddenly remembered—his remains were still in the backseat of my car!

With a chuckle, Jeanie and I realized Dad would have loved being with his two daughters as they talked, walked, laughed, and cried during our unforeseen extra time together. His unexpected "presence" in the backseat of the car was not an accident. It helped to make our unplanned sister time a sacred and precious memory. It's a mental photograph I will never forget.

I will exalt you, LORD,
for you lifted me out of the depths. . . .
Weeping may stay for the night,
but rejoicing comes in the morning.

PSALM 30:1, 5

The Sister with Five Mothers

– Joy Carlson –

Enjoy the little things, for one day you may look back and realize they were the big things.

Robert Brault

My birth was a complete shock to my family. I have sometimes been referred to as "the surprise that wasn't menopause." At age forty-two my mother gave birth to her sixth child and her fifth daughter, which meant I instantly had four older sisters. In truth, it felt more like I had my "real" mom and four additional mothers.

To my surprise, I was never made to feel like an inconvenience. I may have stolen Dad's heart and undoubtedly Mother's lap, but if my sisters ever resented me, they made sure it wasn't obvious. My sisters taught me to enjoy *the little things* in life—and now I realize they were *the big things.*

Mother #1: My real mother is a storyteller and has reminded me by example that many of life's greatest lessons will be learned by my children more easily if they are wrapped in an unforgettable story.

Mother #2: Carol is my oldest sister, and she gave me my

first nephew. She reinforced the value of the "little gifts and letters" I often sent to her son, letting me know that those small acts of kindness produced great encouragement and motivation.

Mother #3: Jennie came next, and she was my "artsy" sister. She brought home fascinating projects from school and took the time to teach me how to make child-sized versions of her wonderful creations. From Jennie I learned how to think outside the box.

Mother #4: Paula (or "Paulie" as I used to call her) spoiled me, and it was wonderful. She was also my Sunday school teacher. For the Christmas program one year, she wanted her class to look their best, so with her own money, she bought green turtlenecks for all the boys and made red velveteen skirts for the girls. I don't know if we all recited our parts perfectly, but we all looked outstanding. Paula taught me that generosity makes people feel valued and significant.

Mother #5: Bonnie was closest to me in age—but still nine years my senior. She had the amazing ability to create something out of virtually nothing. If I couldn't find anything to wear, she was the one who came up with a great outfit from my tired, worn-out separates. If a dress pattern called for three yards of fabric, she could make it look even better out of two. Bonnie taught me how to be creative on a shoestring budget.

Each of my sisters contributed greatly to who I am today

as each mothered me in her own unique way. Today I have seven children of my own, and I'm grateful for learning early that the little things in life are the most important. Carol is the epitome of inspiration and encouragement. Jennie now spends time with my own children with the excess (and love) of a grandmother. Paula showed me how to generously invest in what is precious to me. Bonnie gave me vision, determination, and resourcefulness.

Our relationships have now matured into something more typical of sisters. But I've always had a hard time understanding how some unexpected babies arriving later in their parents' lives grow up feeling unwanted. But then, probably none of them had four big sisters and five wonderful mothers!

Now to him who is able to do immeasurably more than all we ask or imagine, … to him be glory.

EPHESIANS 3:20–21

The Most Prized Possession

– Bonnie Afman Emmorey –

What I spent I lost; what I possessed is left to others;
what I gave away remains with me.

Joseph Addison

During our growing-up years we were actually quite poor—not in the important matters of life, just financially. We were rich in things that really counted, such as love, generosity, and family traditions.

Some traditions were already established by the time I, the fourth sister in the family, arrived. Early on, our creative mother had instituted a wonderful Christmas gift-giving plan. Some years, we didn't have money to spend on gifts for each other, so she encouraged each of us to take our most prized possession and give it to the next sister in line.

Carol, the oldest, was the proud owner of the most beautiful white rabbit fur muff. In the winter, she brought it out every Sunday and wore it with delight to church. Each one of us took turns petting the beautiful fur when it came within our reach. It was definitely her most prized possession, so that year Carol lovingly wrapped it and put it under the tree for our sister Jennie.

How Jennie loved and enjoyed that muff! It was her favorite gift, and she looked forward to Sundays just to have the pleasure of wearing it. It was only in service during cold weather, and when summer came, the muff was carefully stored away.

When summer finally came to an end and the first brisk day dawned, out came the muff and the enjoyment with it. Paula and I would vie to sit next to Jennie for the mere pleasure of petting the furry muff as often as possible. That year when Christmas arrived, Jennie, too, wrapped the muff in holiday trimmings and labeled the gift to the next sister.

Oh, how delighted Paula was when she opened the much-loved, and now a bit worn, white fur muff. Somehow it became even more precious as time passed. I could hardly wait for the next Christmas, because I was almost certain to be next in line for the special gift.

Paula did not disappoint me, and I finally had *my* turn at owning the beautiful white fur muff. It still had the string to go around the neck and felt warm when I tucked my hands inside. The small tear in the lining didn't lessen my enjoyment or pride in being the official owner of the muff.

My year passed far too quickly, and before I knew it, Christmas was right around the corner again. I *knew* the muff was my most prized possession, but the thought of giving it up troubled me. Since I didn't have a younger sister at that time (baby Joy was born nine years after my birth), and Carol and Jennie were getting older and losing their intense interest in the muff, I knew it should go back to Paula—but it was *so* hard. I wrapped the gift, put her name on the tag, and put it under the tree. But it was *too* difficult. I secretly retrieved the gift. I lovingly caressed the now worn fur. It was still so beautiful to my young eyes.

But I knew better. I *had* to give it up! It was my greatest treasure, and it must be given to my sister. I had enjoyed it for a whole year, and my time of ownership had passed. I again wrapped the muff and put a new tag on it with Paula's name in bold letters. Once again, I placed it with care under the tree.

I wish I could tell you how much pleasure Paula had opening her present and seeing the treasured muff. But I can't. You see, on Christmas Eve, I retrieved the muff and decided I couldn't give it up after all. I can't remember what I finally wrapped and *passed off* as a treasure just so I could keep the muff. Not one of my sisters ever said a word to me about my selfishness, and I don't think they looked down on me for not passing it along—but I knew in my heart it was wrong.

Years later, Paula had a Christmas wedding, and each of the sisters wore red-velvet dresses and, instead of flowers, we each carried beautiful white fur muffs. They reminded all of us of past Christmases when we gave each other things we cherished most, and they gave us a new memory to treasure in the future.

Without a doubt, my sisters demonstrated the meaning of true generosity during my growing-up years. I hope my behavior *today* lives up to their example. And if any of them ever needs a kidney, I'll be first in line to be the donor. After all, I *did* keep the muff!

Good will come to those who are generous.

PSALM 112:5

A Changed Heart

– Jolanta Hoffmann –

Chance made us sisters; hearts made us friends.

Anonymous

"How would you like a new sister?" my mom asked one night. "Your dad and I have decided to let Carlisa move in with us for her senior year of high school and to help her go to college."

Carlisa and I were not strangers. We had known each other for several years, ever since she and her four siblings began coming to our downtown church through a bus ministry that picked up kids from the housing projects. All five of them were musically talented, and we sang together in choirs and music ensembles. My family also helped them move from time to time. Carlisa and her sister had even stayed with us for a few weeks after their mother tried to end her life. But I wasn't at all sure about having her become my new "sister." As a self-absorbed sixteen-year-old and the baby of the family, I wasn't eager to alter my status as the only child left at home.

Even though I was apprehensive, I could tell this was

something my kindhearted mom felt God wanted us to do. So I smiled and said, "Sure, that's a great idea."

Carlisa moved her few belongings to the extra bedroom, and we started making our transition from friends to sisters. It wasn't so horrible having her around. I enjoyed having someone to help me with my cleaning chores and to keep me company when my mom and dad went out for the evening.

One day as I walked into the kitchen after school, I heard Carlisa say, "Mom, can you help me with my math homework?"

Then I heard, "Wait until Dad gets home. He's better with math."

I left before either of them noticed me. *Did she say* Mom *and* Dad*? They aren't her mom and dad. They're mine!* I was very resentful every time I heard Carlisa refer to my parents in the very personal way I addressed them. But I didn't let anyone know how I felt.

As the year passed, Carlisa and I spent more time alone together. She began to open up. One day she said, "I like having a dad. My dad left the country when I was very young, and I don't remember him."

I felt embarrassed for not wanting her to call my father *Dad*. My earlier apprehensions were melting into compassion. As we began talking about our early childhood, Carlisa told a story that knocked all of the resentment out of me.

"You're lucky to have such a great mom you can depend on. When I was seven, I had to live in the county parental home because my mom tried to commit suicide. My mom told me she would come back soon. I remember waiting on the bench outside every evening while the other kids were playing—looking for her to come back. She never did. I had to go to a foster home until she got back on her feet."

I was speechless. What kind of response could I give to *this*? I had been acting so selfish. I soon realized there was room for another sister in my life and heart. I could share my mom and dad with someone who had been through so much and had such a great need for security.

I hated to see that year end and have my new sister go away to college. But we weren't through being sisters, even though we no longer lived under the same roof. As the years passed, I celebrated when Carlisa graduated from college. I helped my sister put her wedding together, cried with her when she lost two babies, and rejoiced when she gave birth to two healthy infants.

I'm grateful my mom and dad were willing to open our home and their hearts to another daughter because it gave me the chance to open my heart to another sister—a sister of the heart!

"Whoever welcomes one of these
little children in my name
welcomes me; and whoever
welcomes me does not welcome
me but the one who sent me."

MARK 9:37

This Is What Sisters Do

– Jill Lynnele Gregory –

[Your sister] is your mirror, shining back at you with a world of possibilities. She is your witness, who sees you at your worst and best, and loves you anyway. She is your partner in crime, your midnight companion, someone who knows when you are smiling, even in the dark. She is your teacher, your defense attorney, your personal press agent, even your shrink. Some days, she's the reason you wish you were an only child.

Barbara Alpert

In our growing-up years my sisters and I loved to pretend to be the characters we watched on television. As the youngest, I didn't have much of a choice regarding which person I got to be. Some scenarios were okay, like *The Brady Bunch*. Leanne pretended to be Marcia, Laura took on the role of Jan, and I was Cindy. Or when we watched *Charlie's Angels*, Leanne got the part of Kelly, Laura became Sabrina, and I was, of course—Jill. Other programs weren't as much fun. When *Gilligan's Island* came on, Leanne got to be the glamorous Ginger, Laura was pretty Mary Ann, and my sisters made me be Mrs. Howell. Then there was

Scooby-Doo. Leanne became Daphne, Laura acted out the role of Velma, and I, sad to say, had to be Scooby-Doo—or the guest star, Phyllis Diller—or even one of the Harlem Globetrotters!

Despite my role in real life as the little sister, I maintained a very close relationship with Leanne and Laura. As we have grown into adults, these ties have become deep, strong bonds in my life.

***

When my daughter was diagnosed with autism, my life was turned upside down. One of the strongest anchors during this storm has been the love and support of my sisters. Leanne took on the role of "second mother" in my absence. She cared for my children when I took Sarah to specialists and attended conferences to help me understand my child's challenges. She never complained about the responsibility but saw it as her way to help. She has been my buffer.

When my son was having trouble paying attention in school, Leanne knew my heart could not take on one more burden. She coached him and helped him focus on his schoolwork so he could get back on track. Leanne also recruited help for me when I needed to attend a daily program for three months with my autistic daughter. She prays with me on the phone or stops by with a soda or my favorite flavored cappuccino to encourage me to hang in there.

My other sister, Laura, is a successful manager for a large company. Her job is intense, and she often deals with heavy deadlines and important meetings. As Sarah's therapy required more time than I could give with all the other responsibilities at home, Laura did the most sacrificial thing a sister could do. She stepped down from her position to work part-time so she could assist me with the therapy that Sarah requires.

Each day when Sarah comes home from her preschool for autistic children, Laura comes over to spend the rest of the day working with her. This is not a glamorous job. Sarah uses very few words and often screams or throws objects to demonstrate her disapproval. As unpleasant as it is to admit, she sometimes smears her bowel movements in protest. Sarah has high energy and loves to escape and run away from us. Working with my daughter can be tiring and laborious. But she and Laura have developed a special bond, and Sarah looks forward to her arrival. Sarah's progress has been remarkable! She is speaking words and responding appropriately to questions. I used to cry every time Sarah did something new. Now I am in awe of how God has touched her life with steady progress in a positive direction. Despite my protests my sister will not accept payment for her hours of labor. She simply says, "Jill, this is what sisters do."

How thankful I am for two sisters who continue to play important roles in this unexpected drama in my life. The same sisters I giggled with in our bedroom during our growing-up years are the same sisters who wipe my tears now. I didn't have a choice in selecting my sisters, much like I didn't have the privilege of choosing my television characters when we were playacting as kids, but God knew how much I would need supportive sisters.

I've discovered that sisterhood is a place where needs are known, shared responsibility is embraced, tears are wiped, and joys are celebrated. It's what sisters do.

And my God will meet all your needs
according to the riches of his glory in Christ Jesus.

PHILIPPIANS 4:19

Kitchen Patrol

– Kelly King –

I'll talk all day if you'll only set me going.
Beth says I never know when to stop.

Louisa May Alcott, from *Little Women*

The year I entered seventh grade, my mother accepted her first full-time teaching position. Accustomed to having a mother at home all day, my younger sister and I suddenly found ourselves having to help around the house more often. Although Mom still carried the majority of the cleaning responsibilities, Karen and I had the task of cleaning the kitchen each evening after dinner.

Our family shared a home-cooked meal almost every night. We would gather at the dining room table at about 5:30 p.m., and our southern culture usually dictated the menu. Often the table was piled high with chicken-fried steak, fried chicken, fried okra, or fried potatoes. As tasty as those were, our favorite part was dessert. My mother usually baked homemade pie before she left to teach at the nearby elementary school. Dinner was never complete without dessert, but this also meant extra dirty dishes.

Karen and I soon developed a system for accomplishing our chores quickly so we could pursue other important activities—like watching our favorite television shows. While I cleared the table, Karen became the expert at loading the dishwasher. She could find more room in the dishwasher for an extra glass or skillet than anyone in the family.

Very soon our evening ritual became much more than "kitchen patrol." Our interests were extremely different, and we learned a lot about each other's lives over rinsing glasses and scrubbing gravy out of the saucepan. Karen's popular life was filled with cheerleading, running, and being student council president. I thought my life of piano practice, swimming, and yearbook deadlines paled in comparison to her exhilarating activities. We shared our struggles over friendships, and I secretly envied the attention she received from boys.

During my senior year of high school, the daily kitchen duties took an unexpected turn. Horror of horrors, our dishwasher broke down, and our parents informed us that instead of fixing this appliance or buying a new one, we could just wash the dishes by hand.

We took turns whining, "This is torture!"

I occasionally exploded with self-pity. "In this day and age *no one* washes dishes by hand in suburban middle America!" But we continued washing those dishes by hand. At my side, Karen would wash while I rinsed, dried, and put the dishes back in the cabinets.

Time passed, and we started facing the fact that I would be graduating and heading off to college soon. Our conversations over the kitchen sink deepened as we discussed our futures and what God had planned for our lives. One evening the conversation centered on some special meetings we had attended at church. Karen looked up and asked, "Do you ever question your faith? Do you ever wonder if you really accepted Christ as your Savior?"

I quickly prayed, *Please, God, give me the right words.*

For the next fifteen minutes we discussed how we had both come to know the Lord at a very young age. I recalled sitting next to Karen in church when she leaned toward me and said, "How do I ask Jesus into my heart?"

Being at that time the older, wiser sister at ten years of age, I had helped Karen pray a simple prayer of faith, asking Jesus to be the Lord of her life.

Over dirty dishes I reminded Karen that her prayer had been heard and her commitment to Christ was real. We dismissed the doubts and shared how Christ had been the One who had genuinely cleansed us from our sin. That night, washing dishes seemed effortless as our attention was centered on an intimate conversation between two sisters rather than on completing a mandatory chore.

The following year I returned home from college for a weekend visit. Ready to resume the appointed task, I asked Karen if she had to do the dishes alone while I was away at school. My sister looked at me with a sparkle in her eye.

"I don't have to do the dishes anymore. Mom had someone look at the dishwasher, and he found out nothing was wrong with it the entire time we did those dishes by hand."

We laughed as we recalled the many hours of "slave labor" we had devoted to our kitchen patrol duties. However, deep in our hearts, we knew God planned our time at the kitchen sink for a far greater purpose. Two sisters grew to love each other deeply as they shared their joys, questions, and spiritual concerns at a heart level. Our kitchen patrol was a divine appointment in disguise.

Encourage one another daily,
as long as it is called "Today."

HEBREWS 3:13

A Trip to France

– Nancy Hanna –

An older sister is a friend and defender–a listener, conspirator, a counsellor and a sharer of delights.

Pam Brown

Our *much older* sister, Ginna, was turning fifty, so we decided it was time for an exotic European adventure. My two sisters, two sisters-in-law, and I burned up phone lines in five different cities planning our fantasy trip and a much-needed break from our daily domestic bliss.

When we landed at Charles de Gaulle International Airport, a grin ignited my face, and it didn't burn out for days. The first time I handled money imprinted with the faces of impressionist painters, I knew I had found *my people*. I was giddy with childlike delight and glad I had waited to saunter down the Champs-Élysées and hike up the Eiffel Tower until I was still younger than fifty. Finally I understood the power of the word *wait*. If everything comes too fast or too soon, we don't know the thrill that comes after wanting something for a long time. I sensed God's smile on me as He granted this long-desired heart wish.

For three glorious days we toured Paris. The Eiffel Tower did not disappoint. One evening we toured the city by way of the Seine River—which turned out to be a very energy-conserving way to get our directional bearings. We shopped for silk scarves, tasted crème pastries, and enjoyed an evening of dining at Le Soufflé Restaurant, where lap puppies sat at the feet of their mistresses. We took a day trip to Monet's village of Giverny, and we hiked up to Sacré Coeur to see the lights of Paris twinkle.

The next day, thanks to Martha, our youngest sister, we were off on the fast train from Paris to Marseilles, headed for Aix-en-Provence. We stayed at the real-deal Le Pigonnet Hotel in a bungalow we had all to ourselves. We found ourselves in a postcard-perfect medieval town.

In a flash it was time to return to Paris for one last night on the town. With bags now crammed with French treasures, stomachs cushioned in cream, and wallets emptied of the impressionists—their money, that is—we made our way back to Marseilles to catch the train. Somewhere between the gate and the train, Martha began an earnest search for her return ticket. While the five of us loaded our bags and ourselves onto the train and took our seats, Martha broke out in a cold sweat as she riffled through her books and pockets in search of the missing ticket. When the train pulled out, it became clear there was no ticket.

We were more than halfway to Paris by the time the young man in uniform came through the car to collect our tickets. By now our party had grown tense. He took Lydia's and Kristin's tickets. Ginna gave him hers. There was a lot of *bonjour*-ing and *merci*-ing going on. Martha and I were next. At that moment the "spirit of sisterly compassion and creativity" came upon me. I told Martha to not say a word but only to look sad and nod at whatever I said—to nod *a lot*. She looked at me as if I were some kind of crazy woman (which she already knew was true). Then it was *showtime*!

Having worked in the theater, I knew how to be dramatic. I assumed my "forlorn woman-in-distress" pose and spoke to the man with intensified feminine charm and deep urgency. "We have a problem and I'm sure you can help us solve it ..." I knew, as any actor does, this was my moment on life's stage to play my part most sincerely and with vigor.

"A problem?" said the man in uniform.

I handed him the purchase receipt we found, showing our purchase of five train tickets.

"Ah, yes, as you see by our receipt, we purchased *five*." I pointed to the five of us. "We are traveling together and all of us have our tickets—except for my little sister. She lost hers. I *know* you can help us. In fact, we're leaving France tomorrow, and we're just heartbroken about it."

Without smiling, he said, "Departing tomorrow?"

"*Oui*. We spent all our money, bought many beautiful things, but now we must go." I let the words linger in the air as he weighed his options.

"Well, I suppose if you're leaving tomorrow ..."

"*Oui. Oui,*" I assured him. "And we will have great memories to take home with us."

I tried not to speak my afterthought aloud: *Especially if you let us off the hook for the cost of the ticket.* I wanted to beg, but the new French scarf knotted around my neck gave me the determination to stick to my air of nonchalant confidence in the Parisian style we had observed during our trip.

"If you leave tomorrow then," he said, handing back my ticket with a bit of a scolding look.

"*Merci,* we'll be out of here," I assured him.

And off he went!

Martha shook her head in disbelief at the results of my melodramatic performance. We looked up at three large pairs of sister eyes. "Well?" they asked.

"Done!" I declared.

"*Magnifique!*" they exclaimed.

The American damsels had conquered. As long as we were leaving the country the next day, our lost ticket was forgiven. Though bone-tired from all the fun, I had to grin. God is not only in the center of our small stuff and our quiet needs, He's in the middle of our indulgences as well. *Bonjour!*

Therefore we do not lose heart.
Though outwardly we are wasting away,
yet inwardly we are being renewed day by day.

2 CORINTHIANS 4:16

Timely Advice

– Bonnie Afman Emmorey –

There can be no situation in life in which the conversation of my dear sister will not administer some comfort to me.

Lady Mary Wortley Montagu

It was too soon. I wasn't ready. My son Nathan was only fourteen. How could this have happened?

Nate was a freshman in high school, and the homecoming dance was just around the corner, but I wasn't worried. Nate was way too shy to ask a girl out on a date. We were *years* away from *that* problem.

What I wasn't prepared for was the aggressive girl who asked *him* to take her to this grand event. Without even checking with me, Nate accepted her invitation. I was in a dither! He was too young and innocent.

It was time to call an expert—my sister Carol. She had already been through this first-date and aggressive-girl stuff with *her* son, and she lived to tell about it. Carol would have the wisdom to walk me through this new challenge. I made the call, hoping she would tell me Nate was too young and this date should be canceled. Wrong! She told me that

Nate's peer relationships in his class might be jeopardized if I stepped in and forced him to break the date. This was a very popular girl who had already turned down two other young men before contacting Nathan.

Carol reminded me that Nate and his date were only fourteen, and they would need a driver. Aahhh! That sister of mine was one smart cookie! She suggested that *I* become that driver. Yes, it would mean shuttling a couple of overdressed, underaged, nervous teenagers to and fro, but I would know what was happening at every moment.

Things were going along smoothly when the second shoe fell. They had plans for *after* the dance. They wanted to visit a friend's house to watch a video and have an after-dance party. Whoa! Now I was back to my initial feelings of fear. Nathan was *way* too young! Once again a quick call to my sister was in order.

Carol said, "Bonnie, just ask Nate to call the girl and find out what video they will be watching." Once again, I saw the wisdom in her words. Nate was mortified with my request, but I was unyielding. He knew I was the one who could stop the whole thing, so he broke down and made the call. I overheard him ask the question, making sure his date understood that it was his *mom* who requested the information. Fortunately, the video was one I had seen and approved, so it wasn't a problem; the date plans progressed. Fifteen minutes later the phone rang. It was the mother of Nate's date. She introduced herself to me and said, "When

I heard that Nathan's mother had to know the name of the movie, I knew I was going to like this boy. He must come from a good family." She had been experiencing the same anxieties as me. We had a lovely chat, and both of us felt better about the evening.

The girl I thought might be overly aggressive turned out to be a lovely, reserved young woman. She just knew the type of young man she wanted to date and decided it was worth the risk to make it happen.

The young people enjoyed their evening together. Nate survived his first date, and so did both sets of parents and one concerned Aunt Carol. I'm not sure how many times I called my sister that night as I kept her up-to-date on how the evening was going. But she was there for me. Even though we don't live in the same city, it's good to have a sister who is only a phone call away.

My son Nathan is now well into his twenties, and he feels free to call his Aunt Carol and tell her all about his latest date. I'm no longer the only one to have her on speed dial. We've both learned that God speaks through the wisdom of godly people.

Let the wise listen and add to their learning,
and let the discerning get guidance.

PROVERBS 1:5

The Pine Straw Theater

– Pat Layton –

We don't stop playing because we grow old;
we grow old because we stop playing.

George Bernard Shaw

Every Saturday morning as a young girl, I had a ritual. Before my sisters stirred, I rose early, bursting with creativity, and transformed our front yard into a theater of pine straw, complete with a makeshift stage and ticket booth. Using boat cushions for seating and a tall stick topped with moss for a microphone, I prepared for my performance.

Once my sisters joined, excited for their own theatrical roles, their friends trickled in to join the fun. As the audience settled onto the cozy cushions, I began my presentation. Of course, I captivated the listeners with my speeches, often extolling the virtues of reading or the importance of respecting personal boundaries—especially the boundaries of older siblings.

I relished entertaining my younger sisters, but little did I (or they) know that these childhood theatrics were shaping each of us for our greater purpose.

Each sister had an important role to play:

- As the firstborn daughter, I was the self-proclaimed star of the show and leader of the production.
- The second oldest, my sister Pam, only eleven months younger than me, was always the party girl. She functioned as a one-woman greeting committee, along with providing the warm-up act. Even today, Pam is the group clown of our sister act and continues in her calling as the queen of laughter and joy.
- Our third-youngest sister, Peggy, was and still is the caregiver of us all. Peggy always made sure each guest could see over our barely elevated stage from their low-slung seats. She helped everyone get as comfortable as possible on the moist, dew-covered ground.
- Finally in our "sister quartet" was baby sister Paula. All three of the older sisters constantly bossed her around. Paula did whatever she was asked or ordered to do by her higher-ranking sisters.

Growing up as the eldest, regardless of how "in charge" I appeared, I often felt overshadowed. I never felt like the favorite. It was obvious that our audiences favored my younger siblings. Despite my spirited nature—a feisty blend of assertiveness and independence—I yearned for that sense of being special, of being someone's top pick.

Time passed and the memories of our Pine Straw Theater

produced mixed emotions. As I journeyed through life's heartbreaks and healing, I discovered that what made me special had been there all along, and I began to embrace the unique way God crafted me.

After many "take charge" mistakes, I learned what God said about me and how He planned to use my gifts and talents. Indeed, He *called* me to be a leader and a speaker. My stages became larger as opportunities emerged for speaking about issues I'm passionate about. My support team grew beyond my family and neighborhood. Each performance, whether on a makeshift stage or a grander platform, served as a reminder of God's divine plan.

All four sisters eventually learned to embrace the different women He designed us to be, with all our quirks, flaws, and strengths. We leaned into the intricate tapestry God has meticulously been weaving from the beginning. Through the highs and lows of life's journey, each discovered the truth that she was not a random mistake or afterthought but a deliberate creation, intricately designed by the hands of a loving Creator.

Those Saturday mornings had been more than just childhood sister pastimes—they were glimpses into the gifts God planted within each of us. Every performance, a reminder that even the smallest acts of creativity and expression hold significance in the grand tapestry of God's plan. As we continue to walk this sister journey, we do so with gratitude for the lessons learned on that humble stage of pine straw and with anticipation, knowing there are adventures yet to come.

Today each of us embraces our same roles: Leader, Party Girl, Caregiver, and Baby Sister. And we still play together.

I praise you because I am fearfully and wonderfully made; your works are wonderful, I know that full well.

PSALM 139:14

Joined at the Hip

– Cynthia Reynolds –

Close to my heart you'll always be.
Friends forever, my sister and me.

Unknown

My little brother Darin chuckled as my sister and I walked by with our arms around each other. "You two are always together," he said. "It's like you're joined at the hip!"

My sister Patti and I looked at each other as if we had just received a knock on the door from the Publishers Clearing House spokesman. "Joined at the hip!" we chortled. We bumped hips and swayed through the house in rhythm, trying to walk as close together as possible. No one paid much attention. The fun was all ours.

But we weren't always "joined at the hip." I was seven years old when my sister Patti was born. We called her our little "Patti-cake." As she lay there small and helpless, I wondered if she would ever be big enough to play hopscotch with me or run around on summer evenings catching fireflies as the light of day faded into night in our little town in Iowa. Would she and I ever be friends? I felt very protective of her tiny little hands and feet, her curly golden-brown hair, and her twinkling eyes.

She was not quite two when we moved halfway across the country to California. *That's okay*, I thought. *I'll be able to look after her.* And look after her I did! My mom and dad both needed to work, and I was just old enough to be Patti's babysitter. This arrangement was okay for a while—until I turned twelve—and then my little sister began to seriously cramp my style.

All my friends were taking off for the beach that summer, and I was stuck in a house with no air-conditioning and a five-year-old little sister to watch. I wanted to put on my new two-piece bathing suit, stretch out on my stunning beach towel and check out the boys through my new pink sunglasses. But instead of having fun, I was watching kid shows on TV. Patti was cramping my style—and it was all her fault! I resented having to stay home when I knew I was missing out on all the fun I could have had with my friends.

Then, just about the time Patti was old enough to be on her own, my younger brother was born, and I took care of him too. When I turned nineteen, I was too restless to stay around anymore. It was Patti's turn to be the babysitter! A few years later I married, moved away, and left her. Our parents were struggling, and before long they divorced. Patti was only fourteen. But I had my own life with my wonderful husband. He was studying for the ministry, and we were starting a family and doing overseas missions work. It seemed I had much more important things to do than wait for my sister to grow up.

Three years would passed and I was living in Munich, Germany. The phone rang. It was my mother's voice on the other end of the line. "Patti's had an accident!" My heart stopped momentarily as my mind raced wildly through all kinds of possibilities. "She was cutting the grass and tried to pull a stick out of the lawnmower when her fingers got caught in the blades. The doctor thinks he can reattach her fingers, but there will be nerve damage."

My heart raced at supersonic speed. After hearing more details about the accident and conveying my love and concern to my sister via my mom, I hung up the phone and slumped on the couch. The memory of my sister's baby fingers curling around my thumb sent a wave of pain through my body. *I should be there for her. But would she want me?* The gap between us suddenly seemed to be about *more* than time and space, and it made my heart ache.

I broke down in prayer. "Lord, I am here doing the work You called me to do, but I've missed out on knowing my own sister." My thoughts rambled.

What's she like?

Does she love me?

Does she ever think about me?

Is it too late for me to "be there" for her and to be her friend?

On our next trip to the United States, we went to visit family, and I was nervous. For some reason all I could think about was how mean I had been to Patti so many years ago. I had moved away and never looked back. I walked into her home, and there on the wall was a "sister plaque" I had sent her several years earlier. On the lamp table sat a picture of the two of us; I knew in a heartbeat that we were joined by stronger ties than time and space could ever destroy.

"There you are!" she said exuberantly, rushing across the room with her arms outstretched. I looked into her face and knew she was my Patti-cake. Although time and distance had separated us, we were still joined at the heart.

"Hey, you two," Darin joked, "you *do* separate when you go to the bathroom, don't you?"

It was good to laugh along with everyone else. We were apart for a few minutes—but then we were right back together with our arms around each other, just as we were in days gone by.

I still live far away from my little sister, and her life is burdened with painful troubles I can hardly imagine. But now we communicate more often, and when I hear her voice, I know we are connected—joined at the heart until we can be joined at the hip once again.

"May the Lord keep watch between you and me when we are away from each other."

GENESIS 31:49

Lavish Lips

– Carol Kent –

A smile is a light in the window of your face
that shows that your heart is at home.

Unknown

My sister Paula and I have something special in common, but I never learned the value of our "sameness" until we were almost grown.

It all started in fourth grade. I was sitting in my seat, staring at the front of the classroom, priding myself on being a good student, when I felt a tap on my shoulder.

The young man in the seat behind me was named John, and I'd had a crush on him since the first day of school. He had eyes to die for and all the girls longed for a lingering glance from him. I put on my best smile and lowered my eyes and my voice as I turned and softly said, "Yes?"

I waited. He said nothing. He simply stared at something on my face. His elbow tapped the fellow seated next to him and he said, "Do you see what I mean?"

This student also started staring at something on my face. I heard him respond, "Oh, yeah, I see it."

John, still staring at my face but not directly into my eyes, said, "She *does* have big lips, doesn't she?"

My ego deflated, my heart raced, and I felt a nervous, blotchy rash creep up my neck and publicly announce my humiliation to all the classmates in view of this unpleasant scene. I turned around in my seat and pretended it didn't matter, but I was devastated. I lived through to the end of that painful day and found a quiet seat in the back of the bus.

When the bus pulled up in front of my house, I ran through the front door, charged up the stairs to my bedroom, and wailed like a woman with a broken heart. I was convinced I would never be asked out on a date. I would never get married, because if you don't get dates, you don't get proposals. I was also convinced I would never be hired for gainful employment because of my grotesquely large lips.

My campaign to become one of the thin-lipped people began. I spent hours in front of my vanity mirror taking on the difficult task of rolling my lips in so they would look thinner. The next step was to learn how to speak with skinny lips. This was no small challenge. My words were distorted, and my sisters taunted me with, "What are you doing to your mouth? You look funny and we can't understand you."

I spent several years trying to make my lips smaller and "more beautiful" because of a hurtful comment from a boy in my fourth-grade class. Thankfully, I eventually grew up and my face finally grew into my oversized mouth.

Years later my sister Paula and I laughed out loud as we realized both of us had been "blessed" with large lips. We discovered women were paying big bucks to get collagen injections in their lips, and movie stars like Julia Roberts made big lips fashionable. With a twinkle in her eye and an audible chuckle, my outrageously fun sister suggested, "Maybe we should get our lips tattooed, so when we're little old ladies, we won't have to worry about getting our lip liner on straight."

Actually, that's not a bad idea. However, we have both decided that having a smile on our lips is much more important than the size of our lips!

A cheerful heart brings a smile to your face;
a sad heart makes it hard to get through the day.

PROVERBS 15:13 MSG

A Closet Full of Joy

– Bonnie Afman Emmorey –

A good laugh is sunshine in a house.

William Makepeace Thackeray

When our mother was forty-two, she announced to the family that she was pregnant. All of us were surprised. Mother and Dad already had five children, ranging in age from Carol, who was seventeen years old, down to our only brother, Ben, who had recently turned four. I didn't tell anyone, but I secretly prayed for another boy. That way I would retain my standing as "the baby girl" of the family. It wasn't much, but at least it was better than just being "Daughter #4."

When July came, mother delivered "Daughter #5," and they named her Joy. I wasn't happy. At the tender age of nine, I was jealous of all the attention this darling blonde baby sister was getting from everyone. But over the next several years, my attitude changed dramatically as little "Joy Joy" captured my heart. We often said her first name twice because it described her joy-filled personality so well. Joy and I could always make each other laugh.

***

When Joy began her university studies, I was already an *old* married woman. It was no surprise that beautiful Joy had a string of beaus, but soon tall, handsome Kelly stood out from the rest. Before long, our baby sister fell in love and accepted a proposal from the man of her dreams.

To my surprise, Joy asked *me* to be her matron of honor. My little sister was so busy with her classes that she asked me to plan her wedding. I enthusiastically accepted the assignment. Mother and Dad were in full-time ministry, and they had *five* daughters. Finances were tight. But I was up for the challenge of creating a beautiful wedding on a shoestring budget.

We knew our mother had our grandmother's antique white wedding dress and that her sister (Aunt Kay) had the original bridesmaid's dress. After digging through the closet, we found the wedding dress, and Aunt Kay quickly sent the matching attendant's gown. We decided that with a little effort we could make these dresses work for Joy's wedding. We had a challenge, though—Grandma and her bridesmaid had worn corsets, and each of them had seventeen-inch waistlines. We soon discovered that with new cummerbunds, those dresses would look like they were made for *us*. Joy's beautiful wedding day was filled with old and new memories.

***

As grown-up sisters we continued an earlier passion—shopping—and we've been known to hit resale shops and bargain basements with great gusto. Since Joy's husband is a pastor and she now has seven children, finances are sometimes challenging. One day I was in my closet contemplating the various "sizes of my life" when I got an idea. Joy should come to *my* closet on a shopping trip. I had way too many clothes.

I called Joy and invited her to come on an "all-expense-paid shopping trip"—to my closet. Since I live three hours away and she has a house full of children, we had to plan this shopping trip carefully. Joy and her daughter (my niece, Carol Joy) arrived at eleven at night and we sat around the kitchen table planning our shopping strategy for the next day. We talked, laughed, and reminisced over our many past shopping experiences.

It was time to set the guidelines. It was my closet we would be diving into, and there could be problems. Joy is a very stylish, up-to-date, fashionable woman, and she *has* to be. She has a teenage daughter. My closets are filled with clothes that are more than twenty-five years old. I tend to buy clothes that are a bit unusual, and no one knows *when* or *if* they were ever in style. I have always enjoyed being a trendsetter rather than a fashion follower, and there was a danger of ridicule from my younger sister and her very fashionable daughter. So each of them would be allowed up to, but not to exceed, three laughs. If they passed their limit, the shopping trip would end. They looked dubious, but I was unyielding. My fragile pride was at stake. We finally went to bed and drifted off to sleep.

Morning dawned and the fun began. The closet doors swung open, and the fashion show started. We laughed until tears ran down our cheeks. I soon gave up on counting the laughs. (My little sister tried to be gracious when she found my purple harem pants and the abbreviated matching jacket.) We were making memories, and we both knew it.

Time passes, but one thing remains the same. "Joy Joy" is still living up to the meaning of her name, and she continues to remind me that laughter is the best medicine. Her example helps me to value the memories of the past, to savor our good times together, and to treasure our Christian heritage. And it's no secret—whether in a mall or in the back of a closet, Joy brings much sunshine to our shopping experiences.

I have indeed received much joy and encouragement from your love, because the hearts of the saints have been refreshed through you.

PHILEMON 7 NRSVue

One of My Toughest Choices

– Traci Ausborn –

"For there is no friend like a sister
in calm or stormy weather;
To cheer one on the tedious way,
to fetch one if one goes astray
to lift one if one totters down,
to strengthen whilst one stands."

Christina Rossetti, from "Goblin Market"

"How stupid are you?" my sister asked.

Through sobs I replied, "I guess pretty stupid." It seemed like the thing to do at the time. I was a young married woman with a son almost a year old, and I had a great job. My boss had decided to fly me to one of his offices in North Carolina to see the facility and train staff members. I was excited. It was an opportunity not many young professionals in this company were given.

After weeks of preparation and carefully executed lists, my husband knew when to pick up the baby, what diapers to buy, what phone numbers he could use to reach me, when to feed the dogs, and what days to put the trash out.

I was ready for this trip.

A teary goodbye at the airport gate left me exhausted and wondering why I would put myself through this exasperating anguish for three days of work clear across the country. I walked onto the airplane, said a weak hello to the flight attendant, and found my seat. I was lost in my thoughts when the attendant's voice caught my attention.

"Miss, are you okay?"

I didn't realize I was experiencing a panic attack. I felt like I couldn't breathe. Terror seized me. We hadn't even left the ground yet!

"No!" I gasped.

She motioned to a coworker, requesting assistance. With both of them invading what little air I had around me, I managed to choke out, "I need to get off the plane."

I have no idea how they did it. I don't remember walking down the concourse, but I found myself back where I'd started—at the same spot where I had left my husband and son. But things had changed. My family was gone, and I was no longer breathing freely.

"Should we call 911?" one of the flight attendants asked. "She's turning blue."

I'm certain I was by that point, but I could feel my head beginning to clear.

"No, I'll be fine," I said as reassuringly as possible. "Can you get my luggage off the plane?"

"You're not getting back on the plane?"

Stunned at the thought, I managed a calm, "I don't think so."

Through a series of events still hazy to me, I eventually made it home. Not having the courage to face my boss yet, I needed to talk to my sister. I longed for her listening ear, support, and love.

"You got off the plane?" she asked. "I can't believe you got off the plane. This was a great opportunity for you, and *you got off the plane*?"

Ouch, that hurt. So much for sisterly support!

We talked for several minutes and eventually the shock wore off. I realized my sister loved me enough to ask a question that meant more to me than just the obvious. "Why didn't you want to go?"

I never considered not going, but deep inside I couldn't do it. Her targeted questions launched a soul-searching:

What is it I want to be?

What drives me?

What really matters?

Am I willing to be away from my baby for multiple-day trips to further my career?

Do I need this experience to feel important?

My sister wasn't judging or condemning me; she was just challenging me to look at the motives behind my actions. She loved me in that moment by asking the hard questions and helping me evaluate what really mattered.

I remained at the same company, in that same position,

for ten years. During this time, my boss supported me completely in what was then, and remains today, my first priority—motherhood. He chuckled over the airplane story.

The choice to prioritize my family has kept me close to home. I occasionally speak at conferences and retreats, but I work those events around the sports and school events of my son. This choice has been right for me. My sister knew me well enough to recognize what I hadn't realized yet on the day I made one of my toughest choices on an airplane.

Instead, speaking the truth in love, we will grow to become in every respect the mature body of him who is the head, that is, Christ. From him the whole body, joined and held together by every supporting ligament, grows and builds itself up in love, as each part does its work.

EPHESIANS 4:15–16

Three Sisters and a Butcher Knife

– Page Hughes –

Is solace anywhere more comforting than that in the arms of a sister?

Alice Walker

"But Mom, we're afraid of the dark."

At two, three, and four years of age, my sisters and I had vivid imaginations that played tricks on us when we went to bed. The bushes outside our bedroom windows cast shadows that danced on our walls when the moon was bright. The shadows looked like boogeymen to us, and we often ran to our parents' bedroom, begging them to let us climb into their bed.

"Girls, get back in your bed. You know the Lord is with you, and He is going to take care of you. Remember our verse: 'When I am afraid, I put my trust in you. In God, whose word I praise'" (Psalm 56:3–4).

During those dark, fearful nights, Gina, Dawn, and I would toddle back to bed whispering, "When I am afraid,

I put my trust in you. In God, whose word I praise."

This verse continued to be a comfort to us even as we grew older. One evening when we were young teenagers, Mom and Dad went out for a short time and left us at home. Gina was in charge. As the oldest sister, she was responsible for taking care of the rest of us. The house was locked and we were safe. Then Gina thought she heard a strange sound outside. She ran to get Dawn and me and asked in a hushed whisper, "Did you girls hear anything?"

Wide-eyed with fear, we said, "N–n–n–no."

Gina whispered, "I think someone is out there. Follow me and we'll get away from all of the windows." We quickly and quietly made our way to a corner in the kitchen, a place that wasn't visible from any window. Gina opened a drawer and pulled out a large, sharp butcher knife. Then our big sister instructed us to take turns saying the Bible verse, "When I am afraid, I put my trust in you. In God, whose word I praise."

We carefully followed Gina's instructions and walked around in our tight circle at least four times, taking turns quoting our comfort verse. We then sat down and prayed together, asking God to protect us from whatever adversary waited outside our door.

Within a few minutes Mom and Dad arrived and wondered what in the world we were doing sitting in a circle clutching a butcher knife. We all took a deep breath, relieved and thankful for the presence of our parents.

Mom and Dad chuckled a little but reassured us there was no reason for fear. They were concerned about our use of a knife for protection, but they also encouraged us that we had done the right thing by calling upon God and resting on His word to calm our fears.

Since that evening my sisters and I have had plenty of additional fearful experiences: we've lost children, endured financial stress, and dealt with challenging family relationship issues. Each time one of these fearful situations invades our lives, we go back to the verse we learned as babes, practiced as children, and live by today: "When I am afraid, I put my trust in you. In God, whose word I praise." When we repeat those words, God gives us peace in the middle of life's storms.

The Lord is my light and my salvation—
whom shall I fear? The Lord is the stronghold
of my life—of whom shall I be afraid?

PSALM 27:1

Angel Face

– Carol Kent –

Courage is not the towering oak that sees storms come and go; it is the fragile blossom that opens in the snow.

Alice Mackenzie Swaim

My husband and I had been married for two years when his father and stepmother announced they were going to have a baby. No one had expected another sibling to enter this already very large family. But it didn't take long before all of us were anticipating the birth of this little sister.

Lori came into this world on a day filled with sunshine, and her presence in a room always made the atmosphere brighter. I was sure I saw her smile when she was still an infant, but when you have a vivid imagination (and I do), I admit her "smile" may actually have been a facial contortion caused by a feeling of gas.

As Lori grew, she seemed to have trouble breathing; she coughed and had lung infections frequently. Tests revealed that my five-year-old sister-in-law had an inherited disease called cystic fibrosis that affects the respiratory and digestive systems along with the pancreas and the sebaceous glands. Soon the negative aspects of the disease were wreaking havoc in her tiny body. Her lungs produced thick, sticky mucus that not only kept her from breathing normally but often blocked the bowel and produced great discomfort.

After the diagnosis, Lori began a wide variety of treatments. Sometimes there were debates about whether the *cure* was crueler than the disease. At an early age this lung-wasting disease had to be treated with drugs that produced a barrel chest and huge belly on her little thirty-two-pound body. Lori was always "a little lady," and she struggled with not feeling as pretty as she had once been. The steroids enlarged her face, and the tips of her fingers became like large blue pads.

The disease attacked like a predator, but at the age of eight Lori made a choice. She was determined not to give in to the depression and the discouragement of a terminal illness. Her chipper voice could be heard as she joked with her physicians, "You know, doctor, I'm going to charge *you* for this visit. If you go through with this examination, you'll owe me fifty cents!" The doctors loved Lori and often lingered long after the examinations were completed. Being in her presence was a gift of life and love.

Often Lori would lie on a board, elevated at one end in order to drain her lungs and improve her breathing. Whenever I tried to comfort her, I'd hear Lori's sweet voice say, "Don't worry about it. I'll be okay." She joked with her siblings and joined in the fun of each moment.

As month followed month, her physical condition grew progressively worse. I walked in one afternoon and my then ten-year-old sister-in-law looked up and smiled. "Hi, Carol. I'm so glad you came. I've been talking to God a lot lately and I'll be going to see Him soon."

"What makes you think *that*?" I quipped, with fresh tears clouding my vision.

"I just know," she said with a smile. "It's almost time."

That day there was an angelic glow around this precious child. Her facial expression exuded a quiet confidence that God was in control of her destiny, and even if her life was short, it had been a great ride. I felt comforted and calm as her peaceful spirit positively impacted my own response to her critical condition.

Lori was with her parents on the day God called her home. A smile outlined her lips and Lori's arms were raised upward. It was as if angels had come to carry her safely into the arms of Jesus.

Precious in the sight of the Lord
is the death of his faithful servants.

PSALM 116:15

Christmas Eve Competition

– Bonnie Afman Emmorey –

There is only one pretty child in the world,
and every mother has it.

Chinese proverb

It was Christmas Eve, and we gathered at Mother and Dad's house for our reunion. My four sisters and their families had been coming in at various times all day, and now everyone who could make it had arrived.

The holidays have always been a joyful time of year, and as we added little ones to the Afman family tribe, a new tradition evolved—the Christmas Eve Talent Show, featuring our gifted offspring. All of the young cousins participated, and my sisters and I eagerly watched our children perform. The talents were varied—sometimes our progeny would sing a solo or play a recital piece on the piano. There might be a karate demonstration or a display of artwork. Sometimes a sports video was shown, or a winning medal was displayed.

One year my nephew Josh quoted Luke 2:1–20 from memory, without any coaching. My sister Jennie then shared with pride that he had been asked to recite it in the church Christmas program. That was the same year my son Nathan sang "Skateboardin' Santa." It was spirited and cute, and by the end of the song we were all joining in and singing the refrain right along with Nate. I admit that on some of those Christmas Eves my sisters and I felt some competition as we compared our children's performances. And now it seemed glaringly obvious to me that my sisters were comparing my son's public school education with my nephew's Christian school training.

That night after the talent show, everyone was exhausted but still wide awake with the excitement of Christmas morning just a few hours away. The cousins were all lined up in their sleeping bags on the floor, and we had just finished kissing each face and tucking the children in with love.

One of my sisters said, "Why don't we have the kids all say their bedtime prayers together?"

I experienced a momentary twinge of panic. My children were the only ones not enrolled in a Christian school. *How would my kids' prayers compare to the prayers of their spiritual cousins?* This situation had the potential to make me look pretty bad.

One by one each child prayed. The prayers were all sounding very similar when Jordan, my youngest, had his turn. *He's only four*, I reminded myself. I tried to relax my tense stomach muscles.

Jordan began his prayer, "Jesus ..." (Oh no! What a way

to start! Not even a "*Dear* Jesus.") The knot in my stomach grew tighter.

He continued. "Jesus, tomorrow's Your birthday. Thank You for everything You've done for me all these years."

My sister Jennie turned to me with a smile and whispered, "I want to trade sons." In my heart I did a victory march. *Yes! Yes! Yes!* I couldn't believe it. All of my sisters knew that I had won the prayer competition solidly. I was thrilled! My child had come through in the clutch. I found myself gleefully thinking, *My kid prayed better than* your *kid.*

At that moment as I enjoyed my sister's response to my son's prayer, I wasn't aware of how similar my response was to the proud and arrogant Pharisee (Luke 18:10–14). I'm sure Christ rejoiced in Jordan's innocent conversational tone, but it didn't take long for me to realize my jubilation in winning the prayer competition grieved my Lord deeply. I needed to pray that night, too—a prayer of confession.

The cousins are grown now, but when I'm tempted to compare myself with my sisters or my children with their children, my mind goes back to one Christmas Eve when I learned an important lesson in humility.

For all those who exalt themselves will be humbled, and those who humble themselves will be exalted.

LUKE 18:14

Oh, Bring Us Some Kitty Pudding

–Allison L. Shaw–

Laughter is God's medicine, the most beautiful therapy God ever gave humanity.

Unknown

I am a Canadian citizen who married a California boy and moved far away from home. One of the fringe benefits of marrying my wonderful husband was that I was finally going to have my very own sister! I have two brothers, and my sister-in-law Kelly has two brothers, so this marriage was going to work out well for *both* of us. Kelly had been promoting my addition to the family since she was ten years old, and I was equally excited to have another girl on my family roster.

I adore my in-laws, and I have grown to love California, but at Christmastime I yearn for the holly-and-ivy, snow-filled traditions of my childhood. What I miss the most about spending the holidays at home is my Grandma Marge's Christmas pudding.

Every year we would gather at my grandparents' home for Christmas dinner, and Grandma would always make the pudding. It is a rich dessert for a sophisticated palate, but even as a very young child I adored it. Christmas just isn't Christmas without Grandma's pudding.

And that is why, during my first Shaw Family Christmas in San Diego, I was suddenly homesick for Christmas pudding. I called my grandma to get the recipe and while she was glad to give it, she paused for a moment and then said, "Honey, this isn't really the kind of thing that you *start* on Christmas Eve." But I could not be daunted.

The challenge now was to find suet—on Christmas Eve—in San Diego. For those who are unfamiliar with suet, it's fat. Grandma always used the fat trimmed from around the kidneys of a cow. Since I have known my in-laws since I was sixteen years old, most of my Canadian capers and silly schemes no longer surprise them.

It was while I was on the phone explaining to the butcher at the grocery store that I needed a cup of kidney fat that my new sister-by-marriage, Kelly, walked into the kitchen. Turning to my mother-in-law with a look of horror, she exclaimed, "*Kitty fat?* She's making the pudding with *kitty fat*?"

And thus, my favorite Christmas dish was instantly dubbed "Kitty Pudding." At a moment when I was desperate for a taste of home, my new and much-loved sister, Kelly, reminded me that new memories were ripe for the making. Now if only I could just get the guys to muffle their *meow*-ing as they partake, Christmas dinner would be absolutely purr-fect.

The cheerful heart has a continual feast.

PROVERBS 15:15

The Poinsettia Parade

–Anne Denmark –

Friends are family you choose for yourself.

Unknown

I love Christmas. Celebrating the season has always delighted me to the core of my being. After our family moved to the United States, I initiated a new tradition to share the season with my parents, who were still living in Canada. On the first day of December, I took great delight in ordering a magnificent poinsettia to be delivered to my parents' home. My mom loved decorating for Christmas but had a limited holiday budget. I knew that this bright splash of red would be a joyful start to her holiday season.

Mom would call as soon as the poinsettia arrived and say, "Oh, Anne, it's just beautiful!" She would tell me each little detail about where she would display it, and we would share our plans and dreams for the holiday season. We enjoyed this annual ritual as the kickoff to our Christmas season every year—and each year Mom said the poinsettia was the prettiest one I had ever sent, the prettiest she had ever seen.

But this Christmas was going to be different. The sudden deaths of my mom and dad in the spring of the year had left me broken and numb. This would be the first-ever Christmas without my parents. I knew my precious folks were now smiling from heaven's balcony, but their absence from my life left a lonely chill. I wasn't looking forward to the festivities. I wasn't in the mood for celebration, and I was too weary to pretend. Grief has a way of shutting you down, and I dreaded the familiar memories and family traditions that would only intensify the ache of my loss.

The young married women in the Bible class my husband and I taught knew that I was still working through the deep anguish of losing both of my parents within days of each other. I have no biological sisters, and throughout that spring these friends found tender ways to be like family to me and provide a safe place for my tears. One of these precious women invited me to lunch and listened as I shared stories about my mom, including our Christmas poinsettia tradition.

Her eyes filled with tears as I told her how much I would miss sending the poinsettia and receiving the phone call from my mother. I was thankful to have the summer days ahead of me before the loneliness of the holidays set in.

But life moved on, and I soon forgot about that conversation. When the first day of December arrived, I busied myself doing Saturday morning chores around the house. The doorbell rang and I suspected it might be one of the neighborhood children selling wrapping paper or chocolates for a school fundraiser.

When I opened the door, there stood the young women from our Bible class, each holding a bright-red poinsettia in her arms. They came to honor a beloved tradition. They had not forgotten my sorrow.

That day I experienced the love of sisterhood. Into the poverty of my grieving soul flooded a love that ran deeper than girl talk and friendship. These sisters in Christ entered into my family tradition and gave it back to me as only sisters could.

As my heart surrendered to the impact of their remembrance, I began to sob, "I miss my parents so much." My sisters surrounded me with love, and they wept too. Then the poinsettia parade poured into my home and filled it with the warmth of Christ's love. It was the prettiest display I've ever seen.

Rejoice with those who rejoice;
weep with those who weep.

ROMANS 12:15 NRSVue

A Tent and a Purse Full of Rocks

– Pam Cronk –

When sisters stand shoulder to shoulder, who stands a chance against us?

Pam Brown

I had just earned my bachelor of science degree in elementary education and the summer ahead was filled with promise. In truth, I was looking forward to my first year of teaching in the fall, but summers in the Upper Peninsula of Michigan are exquisitely beautiful, and I thought it was time for an adventure before embarking on my first *real* job in the classroom. My younger sister, Lois, and two cousins (both named Kathy), and I gathered our camping gear and headed for a favorite spot along the shores of crystal-clear Ottawa Lake, not far from our hometown of Iron River.

We had a relaxing week of cooking meals in the great outdoors on a Coleman stove and listening to the loons' calls echoing across the lake each morning. At night the howling of the wolves awakened us at odd hours. We were having a *great* time—playing marathon games of Yahtzee and Aggravation by lamplight, singing our favorite oldies, scaring each other in the dark, and laughing until our sides hurt. In the evenings we sat by our cozy campfire and watched bats dive for bugs. My sister and I were enjoying this time with our cousins.

Midway through the week we went shopping in a resort town about twenty miles away so I could look for some professional clothes for my new job. When we got back to the lake, we decided to go for a refreshing swim before returning to the campsite. I parked my old Chevy in the parking lot, locked the doors, and the four of us went into the changing house. Following a short swim, we grabbed our beach towels and quickly changed into dry clothing.

As we approached the car, I noticed broken glass on the ground. I was amazed to see that the small vent window on the driver's door was broken! "What on earth happened?" I exclaimed. Upon further investigation, we found that my sister's purse was missing, along with a piece of luggage and some clothes I had purchased on our shopping excursion that day.

We had been *robbed*!

My practical sister said, "We'd better call Mom and Dad." So we called home.

Dad was not happy with our news. "Why didn't you lock your things in the trunk, out of sight?" he asked.

The whole evening was filled with questions and

discussions about what had become of our belongings. We didn't report the theft to the police, but we *did* tell the forest ranger, who said other people had reported missing items in the same area. That night we developed a plan for solving the crime.

The next morning we walked along the road leading to the campground, trying to locate anything the thieves might have discarded on their way back to the main road. After checking the roadsides and finding nothing, we turned back.

That afternoon four determined girls schemed to set a trap for the robbers. The plan was to park the car in the same spot and place valuable items inside—including a purse containing rocks for weight. We would leave the items in plain sight with the windows down for easy access. We informed the ranger of our intentions, and he said he would watch from the hillside across from the parking lot.

At the appointed time, Lois drove my car to the beach with our two younger sisters and two young cousins, who were visiting us at the campground. Cousin Kathy and I arrived in her car. We parked both vehicles, and the younger children went swimming.

The "sleuth sisters" and the older cousins then went into the changing house where we could watch the cars from the highly positioned screened windows. The forest ranger was already in place—with his binoculars in hand.

Within minutes, a young man and woman drove into

the parking lot. The man walked toward the picnic table, and the woman approached my car. After looking inside, she gave the man an affirmative nod. She then reached in the window and removed the purse. As she walked toward the man, who was sitting on the picnic table, we dashed out the door of our "changing room position," while the forest ranger ran down from his post. At that moment our mom, dad, and brother Mark, who had been storing bales of hay in the barn, arrived for a swim. Mark's stature as a six-foot-five college football player and the presence of the good-sized forest ranger presented a challenge to the man at the picnic table. He was easily restrained. Someone called the police, and the authorities arrived shortly.

My sister and I were thankful and excited that we were able to solve our own crime with the help of our able cousins. Our local radio station announced, "The state police commend the girls for their actions and bravery." Some months later the criminals were granted their day in court, given the punishment they deserved, and we were able to get back some of our personal items.

As a result of this arrest, other people recovered their stolen belongings, and potential future victims were spared the sense of violation we experienced. My sister and I thanked God for His direction and protection. We will never forget our adventurous vacation with a tent—and a purse full of rocks.

Anyone who has been stealing must
steal no longer, but must work,
doing something useful
with their own hands,
that they may have something
to share with those in need.

EPHESIANS 4:28

Twins Born Four Years Apart

– Carol Kent –

> [A little girl] was notified that a baby brother or sister was on the way. She listened in thoughtful silence, then raised her gaze from her mother's belly to her eyes and said, "Yes, but who will be the *new baby's* mommy?"
>
> Judith Viorst, from *Necessary Losses*

I was an only child for four glorious years. Then Jennie Beth was born. Suddenly my position as the "only" child was usurped by this tiny little bundle of demanding energy that came home from the hospital with my mother and father. It seemed that my mother, who read to me, sang to me, and played games with me, had other, more important things to do, and much of her attention revolved around this new member of our household—*my sister*!

Observing my potential for feeling like a second-place member of the family, my wise mother found creative ways to enlist my help as the "big sister" and gave me important tasks that revolved around caring for my little sister. I ran for diapers, fed her bottles, rocked her, entertained her, and loved her. It didn't take long for me to feel like a significant part of Jennie's life, and a close bond developed. Soon we did everything together and early pictures portray us hand in hand in almost every photograph. We were buddies.

Even though four years separated us in age, we often described each other as "twins" because our interests, hobbies, abilities, and spiritual passions were so similar. We were particularly skilled at finishing each other's sentences, and we had great fun pretending to be the other sister when we answered the phone. People couldn't tell our voices apart.

It was no surprise that as preacher's kids with musical ability, we became a duet team. Jennie's clear, sweet soprano tones were a perfect match for my lower alto harmonies. The music brought us great joy and became an integral part of an expanding retreat and conference ministry we enjoyed together.

As the demands of ministry grew more intense, lengthy practices were required for us to add to our musical repertoire and prepare for ministry commitments. Our *fun* was quickly turning into *hard work*, and all of those practices were more labor intensive than we wanted! Jennie (the more spiritual of the two of us) looked up one day and said, "Carol, when we practice, let's pretend that we are actually singing to God. Let's envision Him right here in this room. We'll have an audience of one, but it will be a very important audience."

This suggestion forever changed our attitude toward practice. We were more energized, purposeful, and focused.

It reduced any feeling of competition or comparison with each other. It reminded us that ministry is about *Him* and not about *us*.

Many years have passed since Jennie Beth became my little sister. I'm still flattered when I pick up the phone at her house and people think it's her voice saying hello. We still describe ourselves as "twins born four years apart." We both grew up to be speakers and authors, and we are encouraged when people say that our written or spoken ministry has helped them find hope. And the thought that still motivates us and keeps our focus in the right place is the knowledge that we are playing to *an audience of one*!

So let's keep focused on that goal, those of us who want everything God has for us. If any of you have something else in mind, something less than total commitment, God will clear your blurred vision—you'll see it yet! Now that we're on the right track, let's stay on it.

PHILIPPIANS 3:15–16 MSG

My Sister's Handiwork

– Bonnie Afman Emmorey –

Thank heavens, the sun has gone in
and I don't have to go out and enjoy it.

Logan Pearsall Smith

"Critically Caucasian." That's what they called me. My husband and I were in the Dominican Republic on a mission trip when that title was first applied by others on our work team. I did look anemic compared to the rest of the population. Somehow the description stuck, even after our return home.

To me it seemed unfair that others around me, even my own family members, could get a tan—and I just burned. I had inherited my grandmother's skin, and it did *not* like the sun. My sister Jennie had inherited skin that would not only tan but also glow at every stage in the process. With our completely Dutch ancestry, how could two sisters have such opposite skin?

One year I tried to get a tan. I went boating with my husband and a friend and came home with second-degree burns covering all of my skin that had been exposed to the sun. The doctor was horrified when he saw me in his office the next day. He said he should take pictures for a medical journal because no one would believe him. That day I learned to be very cautious with my skin. No more tanning for me. I had learned my lesson.

***

Over the years, Jennie and I spent a lot of time together at the beach. My family lived an hour and a half away from where their family vacationed each summer. We drove over for a day trip a couple of times each summer. Of course, she would bask in the sun and enhance her already luscious tan, and I would huddle under the nearest tree, shrub, or umbrella, trying not to expose any flesh.

Jennie would always try to entice me out into the sun, encouraging me to get "just a little." She assured me that it would make me look healthier and less anemic. Since I have been asked if I am an albino, it was tempting. But then I would remember my horrible burn, and sanity would return. "No, umm, no, no, I'm really *enjoying* this shady bush." I looked with longing at the rest of the world out playing in the sunshine.

Then came the summer I decided to venture out. Having decided to take a chance and join in the fun, I had purchased some super-powerful sunscreen. I carefully and completely covered every inch of the front half of my body. Then I flipped over and tossed the sunscreen to Jennie. "Could you help me out? Could you cream my legs and back? I don't want to get burned!"

"Oh, Bonnie, you will look *great* with a little color," Jennie replied. "Sure, I'll cream you."

That day we had so much fun talking, laughing, and enjoying our time together. Confident I was protected, I stayed out in the sun longer than any other time. What I didn't know was how *little* Jennie applied as she lightly glazed her hands over my back and legs.

That evening we changed out of our bathing suits and into shorts so we could walk into town for ice cream. The kids ran ahead, Jennie and I came next, and our husbands brought up the rear. Our husbands' wild laughter caused us to turn around to find out what was so funny.

My husband, Ron, hesitantly said, "Honey, are you aware you have white handprints on the back of your legs?" Graydon, Jennie's husband, was nodding and laughing.

"*What*?" I craned my head around, trying to see the backs of my legs without any assistance of a mirror. "Jennie, what are they talking about?"

At the horrified look on Jennie's face, I knew it was true. "Oh, Bonnie, I tried to apply a light coating of sunscreen so you could get a bit more tan. It looks like I might have missed certain areas. Actually, it appears I missed quite a bit."

The backs of my legs carried visible proof of the power of sunscreen! It was where Jennie's hands landed with more force that the sunscreen actually "took." My sister's handiwork was clear.

I chose to give up shorts for the rest of the summer because that apparel wasn't worth the laughter. After the handprints finally disappeared, I laughed myself. What Jennie did certainly left a mark—but it wasn't permanent. I pray the imprint of Christ on my life is permanent and as visible to those who observe me as my sister's handprints were to our husbands on that hot summer evening.

Your very lives are a letter that anyone can read by just looking at you. Christ himself wrote it—not with ink, but with God's living Spirit; not chiseled into stone, but carved into human lives—and we publish it.

2 CORINTHIANS 3:2–3 MSG

Diapers and Balloons

– Elizabeth Murphy –

How do people make it through life without a sister?

Sara Corpening

It was Saturday night in Cleveland, Ohio, as I sat alone in the hospital with my new baby and my mixed emotions. I was overjoyed at the miracle of birth and the precious little boy who slept in my arms. I was overwhelmed at the thought of taking him home to his thirteen-month-old brother and his busy dad, who spent lots of time traveling for work. Mostly I was overcome with loneliness and the deep emptiness that comes from not being able to share the truly important moments in life with those you love.

My husband, Mike and I had transferred from Raleigh, North Carolina, to a home in Cleveland only two months before Andrew's birth. In the brief time we lived there, my life was more than busy: I lived in a hotel for a month with a one-year-old and two big Labrador retrievers, moved into an old house that needed a makeover, sent my husband on countless business trips, and dealt with finding doctors, hairstylists, banks, babysitters, and grocery stores in a new city. I had no time to make new friends.

Then came news that my younger sister, Susan, only four weeks postpartum after giving birth to her fourth son, had been diagnosed with cancer. My extended family went into a panicked overdrive trying to figure out how to care for her. She was in Dallas—I was *very pregnant* in Cleveland. The focus needed to be on Susan, but I had never felt so helpless, alone, and far from home.

The real estate agent who sold us our house lived in the same area we did and had a daughter of babysitting age. She was the first one we called when I went into labor and had to leave for the hospital. There was literally no one else to watch our one-year-old.

In the midst of Susan's sickness, the birth of our precious Andrew was a bright spot, but one that could only be celebrated via long distance. My heart ached for so much more.

As I settled in for the good, long cry I knew I deserved, I heard a knock on the door and the sound of robust giggles. I couldn't imagine who it could be. Besides my husband, I didn't know anyone in Cleveland who would visit me in the hospital.

The door opened. It was Joan, my Realtor, followed by her three young daughters. The girls were so excited to see a brand-new baby they literally *fell* into my room, filling the space with enthusiasm, joy, and exuberance. They carried a huge package of baby-boy diapers, tied with an equally large bundle of balloons—the biggest and brightest kind.

"We couldn't stay away," Joan said, "but we didn't know if it was okay to come either. Your sister Amy gave us the perfect excuse. Here!" she said as she handed me a card.

My older sister, Amy, had tracked down the only person I knew in Cleveland—my Realtor—and asked her to buy the diapers and balloons and personally deliver them to me in the hospital. This is what the card said:

> Welcome, Baby Andrew!
> Sorry we can't be with you, but we will be so excited to meet you and welcome you to the family. We love you, your mom, dad, and brother too.
> Love, Aunt Amy

No gift could have pleased me more. It wasn't just the package. My room was filled with beautiful flowers from lots of loved ones. It was the presence of a person that touched me so.

Amy knew, in the way only a sister cut from the same cloth could know, that as bad as I felt about Susan's illness, and as much as I knew she needed all of our family to rally around her, I needed them too. She sent me so much more than a present—she sent me a person. That day I was reminded that our creative God sometimes uses Realtors, balloons, diapers, and sisters who are far away to remind us of His love and to lift our heads when we are discouraged, lonely, or downhearted.

But you, Lord, are a shield around me,
my glory, the One who lifts my head high.

PSALM 3:3

The Benefits of Having Blonde Sisters

– Carol Kent –

A blonde went out to her mailbox, looked inside,
closed the door of the box, and went back in the house.
She repeated this action five times. Her neighbor commented:
"You must be expecting a very important letter."
The blonde answered, "No, I'm working on
my computer, and it keeps telling me I have mail."

From www.ahajokes.com

A couple of years ago, I was speaking at an arena event and realized that for the first time in several years, all four of my sisters and my mother would be in the audience. Since I was speaking at a keynote session in front of about six thousand women, I thought it would add variety to the program to have my sisters and mother on the platform during part of my presentation. I asked each of my sisters to share one thing they learned from our mother that they would pass on to the next generation.

Each sister's response was a tender reminder of our

mother's major impact on our lives throughout our most formative years.

- Jennie thanked Mother for being such a remarkable storyteller.
- Paula was grateful that Mother helped her make it through a painful divorce, reminding her that Jesus would never leave her.
- Bonnie reminded us that we often saw our mother on her knees and could hear her praying out loud for us when we came down the big open staircase in the early morning hours.
- Joy acknowledged that Mother helped her make it through a challenging time in her marriage.
- I told the crowd it was my mother who led me to personal faith in Christ when I was only five years old.

As I looked at my four sisters all standing in a row, it suddenly occurred to me that Jennie was a dark brunette. Paula was a very highlighted sunny blonde. Bonnie (a former brunette) was a platinum blonde, Joy's tresses were light brown, and my hair was a vibrant red.

We had all shared serious tributes, but I thought it was time for a little levity. Scanning the crowd, I said, "I'm sure some of you are wondering how the five of us could have come from the same mother with all these varying shades of hair color."

The crowd murmured, and I could hear an audible chuckle. I continued, "Just so you know, except for our mother's and my youngest sister, Joy's, each of these colors is available to you too!" The crowd exploded with laughter.

***

I (the redhead) will be quick to admit that whenever I am with either of "the blonde sisters," I notice they get more attention than I do. When I was younger, I may have been a little jealous, but at this stage of my life, the benefits of having blonde sisters definitely outweigh the negatives. Here are a few reasons why I like hanging out with the blonde sisters:

- We get the best seats in restaurants.
- Strong men immediately help us place our heavy luggage in the overhead compartments on airplanes.
- No one expects us to know the directions to our final destination.
- I don't have the pressure of being the center of attention.
- Women do not find the non-blonde sisters intimidating.
- I have the privilege of helping people understand that my blonde sisters are actually highly intelligent—which makes me feel extremely valuable!

My four sisters and I try to act like mature adults now, but our hair colors are *still* available to you. We figure part of the fun of life is to keep people guessing which of us is the oldest, and we plan to delay "the graying of America" as long as we can hold out.

Since blondes have more fun, we all plan to end up in the same retirement village someday. However, the main reason we'd like to be together is the bond of sisterhood that connects us at the heart level. We have shared laughter, tears, family crises, graduations, weddings, birthdays, and funerals. And we know that being sisters has strengthened us in a way that goes much deeper than visible "roots."

A cheerful disposition is good for your health;
gloom and doom leave you bone-tired.

PROVERBS 17:22 MSG

My Sister's Defender

– Jill Lynnele Gregory –

Sisterhood is powerful.

Robin Morgan

It was one of the most exciting days of my life. My sister was due for delivery. Leanne desperately wanted to be a mom. After struggling through years of infertility, she had finally become pregnant—not with just one baby, but with *two*!

The twins were scheduled for a C-section at thirty-six weeks, but on the day prior to the scheduled surgery, Leanne's blood pressure soared. Following additional blood work, the doctor concluded my sister had a condition known as preeclampsia (hypertension and a buildup of fluid). The C-section needed to be done immediately.

Leanne went into the hospital and all of us experienced sheer exhilaration as she gave birth to two tiny, beautiful baby boys. But moments later our joyful celebration turned into unspeakable fear. Complications set in. Doctors were using unfamiliar terms, and my mind was swirling as someone explained that Leanne's organs were shutting down and her life was in danger. Three blood transfusions were given to my sister, and we waited for word on her condition. I begged God to let her live.

The turning point in my sister's recovery was the day her husband asked if the twins could be taken out of the neonatal intensive care unit and brought to her. My brother-in-law knew Leanne needed to see the boys so she would have a visual image of why she needed to fight for her life. Soon after that she started sitting up, and eventually she was able to walk again. Finally the hospital sent her home, but her twin sons remained in the NICU.

Leanne wanted to bond with her babies and went to the hospital during the feeding times. Normally she would show her sons' ID bracelets on her wrists and the guard would allow her to pass the security desk and go directly to the elevator. Since she did this on a daily basis, the guards knew her and just waved her past the security checkpoint.

Leanne was still very frail one day when I helped her enter the hospital. From his seat behind a high counter, a guard I had never seen before stopped her. Leanne showed him the ID bracelets and explained that she was at the hospital to feed her twins. He flashed her a mean look and told her she was not allowed past him without a hospital pass. She explained that she had never had to get a hospital pass before and had been instructed to show the twins' ID bracelets when she needed to get in to feed her babies.

He glared down at her from his powerful perch and said with disgust, "I don't care what you've done in the past. You'll have to go down the hall and get a hospital pass today!"

My sister was very weak but managed a reply. "Yes, but sir, I've never needed a pass, just the twins' ID bracelets—"

Before she could finish her sentence, the guard blurted, "I don't care what you've done before! *Get a pass!*" Then, with a smug look on his face, he did one of those rolling wrist gestures that ended with a finger pointing to the nurse's station down the hall. Leanne was flustered and upset. So was I.

His demeanor was nothing short of cruel. I was born a redhead, and my feisty spirit has remained strong. The anger that arose in me as I observed this man demean my sister in her exhausted and weakened state is hard to describe.

With tears in her eyes, Leanne slowly turned and shuffled down the hall. I stopped her. "No, Leanne, you sit here. You are in no shape to run through this hospital to get a pass. I'll get it." I sat her down in a chair and walked to the end of the hall to the nurse's station.

I fumed as I waited. When my turn came, I inquired, "Pardon. Does my sister need a pass to feed her twins today?"

The nurse looked over, saw Leanne, and immediately waved to her. "No, she's fine. She can go right up to the neonatal intensive care unit."

Pointing my finger down the hall, I said, "That guard won't let her through." The guard with the attitude glared back at me.

The nurse shouted down the long hallway, "Hey! Let her through. She's okay."

As I stormed back down the hall, the guard approached my sister. Suddenly words came out of my mouth that surprised me: "Don't you talk to her! Leave her alone!" I grabbed Leanne and tried to shield her from the cold-hearted guard.

He started backpedaling. "Hey, look, I was only doing my job, and I don't usually work this post."

"Sir," I said, "that gives you no right to talk to someone in such a demeaning way."

I ushered Leanne into the elevator. As we made our way up several floors, my sister had tears in her eyes. "Thank you," she said softly. "That guard was so mean. I just didn't have the strength to fight him." Then she smiled. "I have never seen you so angry. You are really scary when you're that upset." We hugged and realized we could finally laugh out loud as we slowly made our way to the twins.

Several years have passed since I protected Leanne in that hospital corridor. I still love being there for her when she needs me, and I know she'll do the same for me when the tables are turned. After all, we're sisters!

Jonathan was deeply impressed with David—
an immediate bond was forged between them.
He became totally committed to David. From that
point on he would be David's number-one advocate.

1 SAMUEL 18:1 MSG

A Memorable Road Trip

– Bonnie Afman Emmorey –

Laughter need not be cut out of anything,
since it improves everything.

James Thurber

It was a bitterly cold night. Carol and I were on our way home from teaching a seminar in Indianapolis, and we had a very long road trip ahead of us. The drive started out normally enough, but the farther we traveled, the more we needed to do creative brainstorming to make the miles go by more quickly.

Somehow we ended up on the subject of death, and while ordinarily it's not a humorous subject, that night we were just tired enough to find the laughter in this usually somber theme. I could just picture Carol being fitted for her heavenly gown and angelic wings.

We decided to use the next hour to plan out our own funerals. To some this may seem morbid, but since Carol and I are ready to face eternity with joy and our family *loves* a gathering of any sort, planning our homegoing celebrations seemed like an appropriate use of time on this trek home.

With laughter punctuating every idea, we made lists of favorite family foods that could be served, and we decided the event definitely called for great music. We figured if the family was getting together anyway, they might as well have a fabulous meal and extraordinary entertainment. Our exhaustion added to the combined hilarity and absurdity of the moment.

Suddenly Carol quit laughing and took me by surprise as she paused a moment and very seriously asked, "Bonnie, if I go first, will you do my eulogy?"

Her sincere demeanor stunned me momentarily, and I came face to face with a fact of my life. I lose control when I am at funerals. I might not even know the deceased personally, but show me a dead body in a box, and I go to pieces. Totally out of control.

Because Carol is not just my sister but also one of my all-time favorite people, I was honored to think that she wanted *me* to do her eulogy. But I had a disturbing vision of me at that memorial service—bulbous red nose streaming, tissue box in hand, hiccupping erratically as I tried to speak.

It was clear to me that she was having difficulty understanding my dilemma. This is a woman who has made "being appropriate" a fine art. It would be difficult to find a more politically correct, perfectly coiffed, classically dressed, and poised-at-all-times woman. The image of my blotched face and tattered tissues returned.

But within moments Carol came up with the perfect

solution. She blurted, "You could do lip-synching!" She suggested I tape the audio ahead of time and just move my lips during the service. We howled with laughter. Carol thought people would be touched by my emotion because tears are very appropriate at a funeral. She could picture it all—my voice speaking eloquently while I dabbed a tear from the corner of my eye. Her beautiful, tasteful picture of this event and my nightmarish version were not even close!

That night we laughed until we cried, and I realized anew how blessed I am to have a sister like Carol.

Since memorial services are technically for the ones left behind, I've decided to start a new tradition—a *living* eulogy. This way Carol can know what I'll be lip-synching at her service.

> Carol, you are a rare and beautiful woman. Your inner beauty is as vivid as your outer shell, and the combination is a two-part harmony that fills any room with sweet music. People are drawn to you because of your "calm and gentle spirit, a thing very precious in the eyes of God" (1 Peter 3:4 PHILLIPS).
>
> Many people will be in the kingdom of heaven because you wisely used the gifts you were given. Not only did you use your own gifts, you *multiplied* them as you trained others in ministry. Your words are as "apples of gold in settings of silver" (Proverbs 25:11).
>
> You are my beloved sister. You make family

reunions a celebration. You are my dear friend. You know how to keep a secret. You are my beloved mentor. No one could be a more Christlike woman. I love you.

Our road trip finally came to an end. We had laughed hard and loved much. I am sadly aware that there is no way I could ever make it through my sister's eulogy—even lip-synching.

So here's the deal, Carol. I'll go first and you can do *my* eulogy. No, wait a minute. Let's go together and have the great joy of hearing our welcome-home greetings from our Lord Himself.

Now there is in store for me the crown of righteousness, which the Lord, the righteous Judge, will award to me on that day—and not only to me, but also to all who have longed for his appearing.

2 TIMOTHY 4:8

Sisters Who Understand

–Toni Schirico Horras–

Sisters function as safety nets in a chaotic world simply by being there for each other.

Carol Saline, from *Sisters*

My sisters and I were busy assembling dinner in the church kitchen when the overhead speaker indicated the worship music had ended in the sanctuary and the pastor was about to lead the congregation in a time of prayer. Suddenly my sisters stopped in the middle of their work and looked in my direction.

One precious friend spoke up. "Pastor is going to pray for Jared today. Let's stop our work and pray too." We found each other's hands and stood in a circle. I realized in that moment I had been trying to bury my pain by staying busy. Helping to prepare for this dinner kept the focus off my aching heart. One by one I listened as these closer-than-family sisters prayed for me and for my wayward son.

When my husband and I first adopted transracially over seventeen years ago, I began to pray for friends of color. I wanted girlfriends, sisters! I wanted peers to help me understand what I couldn't possibly comprehend growing up in my white skin. I wanted to be confronted when I was wrong and set straight. I didn't want my two adopted African American sons to be disadvantaged because they had a Caucasian mother.

It was a bold and ignorant prayer. But over time God answered. Some of my prayed-for friends were in that kitchen; many were in other parts of the church, and others were scattered across the country. One of my dear friends nicknamed me "Sistah-girl," which I received as a high compliment.

Each one understands my heartache too well. Many are grandmas; some are my age and grandmas many times over. One woman has watched her brother live a playboy's life, father a child, and still "act a fool." Another had a son leave home for weeks only to wake up one wintry morning to find him curled up asleep on her front stoop—repentant and hungry. Many have sons in prison; one has had two incarcerated sons at once. Another has a daughter on her third child out of wedlock—and my dear sister loves those babies with all her might. Several have sons lost to the streets—whereabouts unknown. And yet another has a son who was murdered. She wears a locket around her neck with his picture inside. Others blessedly have sons who love God with all their hearts and have not succumbed to temptation.

These were the sisters who felt my pain and loved me

enough to boldly beseech God's throne for me that day. I could tell by how they prayed they had "been there" for their own loved ones many times. Tears flowed. How immensely good of God to surround me with this depth of understanding! How silly of me to think I would be spared this pain when none of them had been. How could I have thought I would sidestep this trial when each of their sons and brothers had to face all the same temptations my son had. How high and mighty of me to ever think I might escape this challenge!

When I first asked God for friends of color, I thought it was to benefit my sons. And it has—but not nearly as much as it has benefited me. How like God to draw us into something that makes sense to our human way of thinking and then turn it completely around to teach us things He wants us to learn.

And that is just what is happening with my wayward son. He thinks he is running away from us and away from all things white and middle class to authentic blackness. He thinks the restlessness he feels is because he is not really "black enough." He attributes the angst to his adoption and being "taken away from his people."

When will he come home, look around, and see these loving, generous, and godly people he rejected? I have no idea when the lightbulb will go on in his mind and heart, but I pray he'll come home soon and make up for lost time. I long to experience the years the locusts have eaten. I wasn't finished with mothering this son. Meanwhile, I will trust God and lean on the support of my knowledgeable, experienced "been there, done that" sisters!

Let perseverance finish its work so that you may be mature and complete, not lacking anything. If any of you lacks wisdom, you should ask God, who gives generously to all without finding fault, and it will be given to you.

JAMES 1:4–5

The "Healing" Quilt

– Anne Denmark –

The only gift is a portion of thyself.

Ralph Waldo Emerson, from "Gifts"

At 4:45 p.m. on February 1, 2003, I was crushed between life and death, wondering if I would ever take another breath. It was my husband, Don's, fifty-second birthday. To celebrate we had flown to Muncie, Indiana, to participate in Parents' Weekend for the Ball State University volleyball team. Our son was a senior on the team, and we had just left the luncheon banquet with Matthew and the student trainer, Mike, when a truck struck our rental car from behind. The first impact crushed my back and my scapula, clavicle, sternum, and ribs. Our car then veered into oncoming traffic and collided with an SUV, breaking Don's shoulder and pinning his leg under the dashboard. Matthew and Mike were able to get out of the car and get help.

Our birthday celebration turned into an all-night visit to the emergency room and ultimately into a time of prayerful thanksgiving for spared lives. For me, that evening was also the beginning of an eleven-day hospital stay and months of painful recovery, which required me to wear a restricting back brace and bone stimulator.

The injuries put frustrating limits on my active life. Each morning I would wake to another day totally reliant on others to bathe, dress, and roll me into the body brace. It was humbling to be so helpless. It was humbling to need so much help. Day after day my only job was to wait and heal. Sometimes the hours of pain chipped away at me until discouragement clouded my thoughts. *Would I ever get better?*

News of our accident resulted in an unbelievable outpouring of long-distance love from Don's mother and three sisters. Several weeks after we returned to our home in Oklahoma, a large box containing a handmade quilt arrived at our door. As I unfolded the gift, a cheerful array of color spilled over my lap. Tucked inside was a letter from my sister-in-law Kathy sharing the story behind the quilt. It began with her prayer, and I read it through tears of joy.

> "Lord, my sister-in-law is hurting, and I want her to know how much she is loved. It's so hard to be so far away—to feel so helpless."
> *Make her a quilt.*
> "A quilt, Lord? But I'm just a beginner ..."
> *A quilt, Kathy. Others will help.*

That handmade quilt, was a constant reminder of the fact that I was loved, prayed for, and supported.

Praise be to the God and Father
of our Lord Jesus Christ,
the Father of compassion
and the God of all comfort,
who comforts us in all our troubles.

2 CORINTHIANS 1:3–4

Soul Sisters by Choice

– Cynthia Spell –

A friend is someone who knows the song in your heart and can sing it back to you when you have forgotten the words.

Unknown

When I found out my grandparents' home was going to be torn down, I contacted the current owner and asked if I could walk through the house one last time and search the yard for any of my Nana's flower bulbs. He graciously agreed. My lifelong friend Dawn was more than happy to join me. Standing in the empty, dilapidated house, loving memories overwhelmed me, and Dawn wrapped her arms around me as I shed a few sweet tears.

Walking outside, we were delighted to find a patch of huge paperwhite daffodils blooming! One thing we share is a love for flowers, and although we are professionals when it comes to digging in the dirt, we quickly realized we had a problem. The bulbs were almost as big as my fist and held captive under a mass of wisteria roots.

"I didn't bring the right tools for this, so it's going to take a lot of work," I said. "Are you up for it?"

Dawn laughed. "We always say we can do hard things as long as we do it together. So let's leave no bulb behind!"

It's a good thing no one was there to film us as we grunted and groaned while fighting to separate the large roots. Stopping to rest, we realized we were both covered in dirt from our battle to free those tangled bulbs. "I wonder how many truckloads of dirt we've moved together," she said with a grin.

I wiped the sweat and mud off of her cheek. "Do you mean literal dirt or figurative dirt? Because in all the years I've known you, we've transplanted flowers in five different states, but we've also dealt with the dirty mess of emotional trauma, physical illness, spiritual trials, and plenty of disappointments and losses."

"You're right," she said. "Every major event in my adult life involved you, through the good, the bad, and the ugly."

Dawn and I met when we were freshmen in college. We were both wounded young women in need of a friend. God surely smiled when we met because He knew what a treasured gift He had just given us. For forty years, our lives have been woven together like a tapestry. Our journey together has included unanticipated twists and turns, mountains and valleys, joys and sorrows.

I imagine a picture of our tapestry where some scenes are intertwined in vibrant, joyful colors when we celebrated the births of our children. Different parts of our life stories, like betrayals and divorces, are a tear-stained disarray of tangled grays and black. In hindsight, I can almost see the invisible bond two young girls formed when they needed each other most. I can trace the paths we've traveled together, offering the support and love we both needed.

"What's your favorite thing about our friendship?" I asked her.

"Oh my goodness, what a big question! Where do I even begin? My life is better because of the way you always listen with your heart and offer me understanding and acceptance. You know my love language is 'words of affirmation' and go out of your way to shower me with encouragement. But I guess more than anything, I love the bond of trust we share and the way it only strengthens with time." She smiled. "It's a bonus that we are the president of each other's fan club."

"I'm almost embarrassed to admit I've just had an epiphany about our friendship," I said. "My whole life I've bemoaned the fact that I didn't have a sister, but you've been right here, walking through every step of life with me. We've been closer than most sisters ever could be. I've always called you my heart friend, but today I realize that in you, God blessed me with a sister of my soul."

We sat together in the dirt while happy, muddy tears ran down our faces, and we rejoiced over the goodness of God in our enduring relationship. My precious sister isn't related to me by DNA, but we are bound together by the love of two committed hearts.

Spring is here, and Nana's daffodils are proudly showing off their first blooms. Knowing it would make Dawn happy, I took a picture and texted it to her. "Look what just popped out of the ground."

The blossoms are the sweet reward of our work to free the bulbs that seemed hopelessly trapped in those roots. I smiled, remembering that God is like a master gardener. He never leaves us stuck in life's hard places. He is always in the process of setting us free and redeeming the beauty in our lives. I'm so thankful He blessed me with a "soul sister" to share the journey.

I thank my God always .... For I have had great joy and comfort in your love.

PHILEMON 1:4, 7 NASB

Thanksgiving Blessings

– Traci Ausborn –

Sisters make the bad times good
and the good times unforgettable.

Helen Bryan

It was going to be a strange Thanksgiving. Our parents were over twelve hours away on their annual fall pilgrimage to Reno, Nevada. They were always home by Thanksgiving, but this year they'd gotten caught in one of the worst snowstorms to hit the Sierra Nevada range.

When we learned Mom and Dad were snowed in, the original plan had been to spend Thanksgiving with my oldest sister's in-laws. They were like a second family to me, and it was always fun to spend time there.

But there was another problem: my brother-in-law had been recently diagnosed with leukemia. I wasn't prepared for the call I got from my oldest sister on Thanksgiving morning.

"He's not doing well, kiddo. We have to go to Seattle," she said.

Seattle was the best and closest option for treatment, and

thankfully, the storm our parents were stuck in wouldn't hamper my sister's travels.

Instead of spending Thanksgiving with my parents, my sister, or her in-laws, I was literally stuck in the middle of a ten-acre ranch with my middle-sister who never liked me—just because I was born.

My oldest sister hadn't just called to update me on my brother-in-law, she had called to coach me through prep for Thanksgiving. "You can handle this, right?" she asked.

"Sure, no problem," I responded with as much moxie as my scared eleven-year-old body could muster.

"You've got the turkey and all the trimmings," my sister said. "I even made your favorite fruit salad. I'm sorry I won't be there." Truth be told, I could live happily on my sister's fruit salad.

"You have to cook the turkey, though. Follow the directions I left for you ... and you can always ask you know who to help."

I knew she meant our middle sister. "She burns boiling water," I said flatly, repeating a well-known family fact.

"You can do this. I'll call you when I get to Seattle." With that, my oldest sister hung up the phone, and then my fifteen-year-old sister and I were officially left to fend for ourselves on Thanksgiving Day. To say I was disappointed was an understatement.

I went to tell my sister the news.

"She's going to Seattle?" my sister asked.

"Yeah ..." I wasn't sure what was coming.

"Mom hasn't called?" Whenever our parents landed for the night, Mom would always call from the hotel to give us the number where they were staying, since this was long before cell phones and the internet.

"Nope."

"Hmm ..." she breathed. "This doesn't feel much like Thanksgiving, does it?" It was true; the house was painfully quiet—no parents, no oldest sister, no niece, no nephew.

"We have a turkey and all the other stuff," I said hesitantly. "We can cook it."

"Really? Are you kidding?"

My confidence was building. "Sure. I've watched Mom do it hundreds of times." A bit of exaggeration from a preteen for sure, but I was slowly winning her support.

She actually smiled. "Okay, I'll help."

"I think the turkey takes a long time to cook, so let's prepare that first." Together we pulled the turkey from the fridge. I read the instructions our oldest sister left, did the best I could to remember what I'd seen Mom do, and soon the turkey we nicknamed Tom was in the oven.

My sister found the Thanksgiving parade on TV while I gathered the rest of the traditional ingredients. We opted for our favorites—potatoes, gravy, fruit salad, canned corn, boxed stuffing, jellied cranberry sauce, and two cans of olives because they were my sister's favorite. We agreed that the green beans and yams could go back to the pantry.

I did wonder, though, where the turkey parts were. Every year, my dad insisted on frying those up himself, and no one else would touch them. He'd be disappointed this turkey didn't come with any, but he wasn't here, and I certainly didn't know how to cook them. Perhaps this was best.

Working together, we peeled the potatoes, drained the olives, and put the cranberry sauce on Mom's special serving plate. I made the gravy and stuffing (my mother had an awesome cookbook with instructions even an eleven-year-old could follow). For the first time in memory, my middle sister and I did something together without nearly killing each other. We had no idea what we were doing, but we did it—imperfectly—together.

Just as we were sitting down at the table, a car pulled up. Our parents! They made it home safely—and just in time for the meal. Truly a Thanksgiving blessing.

***

"This was a great meal, girls," Dad said.

"Yes, it was," Mom interjected, "but who's cleaning up the mess?"

My sister and I looked at each other. Much to my parents' surprise, she said, "We'll do it together."

I have to say I was pretty full of myself. At eleven, I'd cooked a pretty good Thanksgiving meal. My sister and I worked well together, and my parents got home safely.

But moments of victory tend to be fleeting. A big head was not in the Lord's plan for me. As Mom worked to remove the remaining meat from the bird, she smiled. Reaching into the turkey, she pulled out what looked like a bag. "You missed the giblets."

My sister laughed. "I wondered where those were!"

I was mortified and totally deflated. Tears filled my eyes.

Affectionately my middle sister patted me on the shoulder. "Bet you'll never do that again."

She was right.

I can do all this through
him who gives me strength.

PHILIPPIANS 4:13

Bunny Hill Sunshine

– Jennie Afman Dimkoff –

Seize the day!

Saul Bellow

"That *does* sound like fun, Carol. The kids would love it. All right, we'll go!" I couldn't resist Carol, who was using her considerable motivational skill to convince me that a ski trip would be a great way for our families to spend time together. Hanging up, I stared at the phone. What had I committed to? The last time I'd gone skiing was in high school when I'd come home with a sprained ankle after crashing into the lodge.

In preparation for the trip, I went outlet-mall shopping, buying our entire family ski pants. For myself, I purchased a lovely ensemble in teal, black, and fuchsia. I knew Carol's ski suit was light turquoise, and we would coordinate beautifully. (I was certain that *looking* like a skier was the first step to *being* a skier.)

Upon checking in at the resort, we decided to make reservations for dinner at seven and take advantage of the beautiful, sunny afternoon to go cross-country skiing. "It really is easy," Carol assured me, "and we'll be able to talk all along the way."

There were six of us when we started out. Carol's son had opted for hitting the daredevil downhill slopes, but our husbands and my two children were with us. Caught up in conversation, Carol and I fell to the rear of the group, taking our time. A natural encourager, Carol was drawing me out about recent ministry experiences, and our time together was precious.

An hour later, the kids announced that they were going on ahead, so we waved goodbye and fell back into deep conversation. Suddenly we realized our husbands were out of sight as well. Calling out to no avail, we took a shortcut back to the lodge. My muscles were already screaming, and I longed for a hot bath before dinner.

Five hours later, we still had not reached the lodge. Soon it would be dark. I was close to tears, and Carol's "I don't understand how we managed to get so *far* from civilization" comment was no comfort. I had taken off my skis two hours earlier and was lugging the expensive rental property, sorely tempted to throw it aside as I stumbled along. "Downhill skiing is much easier than this, Jennie," Carol assured me. "I'm amazed that this trail is so rough and uneven."

She had no sooner made that comment when I noticed a marker along the trial. "Carol, what does that black diamond shape on that sign mean?"

We were lost on the roughest trail we could have chosen!

"I want to just lie down and sleep for a while," I whined. Carol insisted we keep going.

The sunset was beautiful, but I missed its majesty, thinking only of impending nightfall and the fact that the temperature was dropping rapidly. Coming to a halt, Carol turned toward me, her breath emerging in frosty puffs. "I think we should pray, Jennie. God knows where we are, even if we don't."

Two colorful amateur skiers bowed their heads and pleaded with God for help.

"Helloooo!" Lifting our heads and turning in the direction of the voice, we saw a lone skier waving at us. Certain our prayers had been answered immediately, we waved back wildly, only to be disappointed. Although he was a far better skier than we were, he was lost too, and he was rapidly dehydrating. Still, his presence was a comfort.

We managed to climb a steep embankment to a beautiful house, but we banged repeatedly on the door to no avail. We actually considered breaking a window of the luxurious place, sure that a burglar alarm would go off and we would be rescued, but the thought of vandalism charges held us back. The house seemed to be on a narrow, deserted lane. Having no idea where it led, we decided to get back on the ski trail, certain that it would lead to the lodge and to our husbands, *who should have been out looking for us*!

In the fading light we finally spotted a large house on a hill in the distance. Our spirits rose as we climbed the embankment and saw vehicles lining the driveway. The homeowner was not gracious, but one of her guests offered to drive us to the lodge several miles away, where our very worried husbands met us with open arms. They hurried to notify the ski patrol that we were back.

The next morning, I awoke with a painful groan to the ringing of the phone. "Good morning, dear sister!" sang Carol. "I've signed us up for beginner lessons on the bunny hill. Meet me for breakfast in thirty minutes and we'll hit the slopes at ten!"

Sister Sunshine had lovingly motivated me once again.

Gently encourage the stragglers,
and reach out for the exhausted,
pulling them to their feet.
Be patient with each person,
attentive to individual needs.

1 THESSALONIANS 5:14 MSG

A Matter of Perspective

– Bonnie Afman Emmorey –

If you judge people, you have no time to love them.

Mother Teresa

It was December, and family was coming to my house for the holiday celebration. Little did I know that something important, even life-changing, was going to happen to me during that reunion.

The event took place on the day after Christmas. My mother, two of my sisters, and I decided to go into town to the coffee shop where we would later meet up with our husbands. The guys, all bundled up in their winter gear, had run into town through the woods behind our house, but we drove the three miles to town. Mother, Carol, Jennie, and I sat in one booth chatting over our coffee and tea, eating delicious peanut butter cinnamon rolls while the guys took over another section of the restaurant. We laughed and chatted, savoring our time together, knowing that before long everyone would be headed for their various homes.

We left Joy, our youngest sister and the main topic of our discussion, home playing with the nieces and nephews. Joy was in her late teens—beautiful, talented, intelligent, and very much pursued by several young men. That morning, we were discussing her beaus, listing their positive virtues, or their lack of admirable traits, and generally evaluating which boyfriend we thought would fit into our family best.

One name came up, and I burst in with my evaluation. "He's *so egotistical*." Unfortunately, I had never even met the man, but I was putting him down based on something I once heard someone say.

Quietly from beside me, my sister Jennie said, "Well, he *does* have a healthy self-esteem."

My heart was pierced!

We had basically said the same thing, just from opposite perspectives—negative and positive. The conversation continued to the next prospective boyfriend. No one else was aware of it, but I had just encountered one of those soul-baring moments. It wasn't the only time I had chosen a judgmental word over an affirming word.

It was frightening to me as I realized that I had allowed myself to slowly sink into being a negative, critical person. At that time, my sons were young, and my example would shape their opinions and attitudes. Mine was the pattern they observed daily.

After my sisters and their families left that day, I faced my problem. I had been choosing to live in a negative world when I didn't have to. The choice was mine. I knew that my perspective was just that—a perspective. My husband, Ron, and I often laughed about this very thing. I once made the comment that his sports car "drove like a truck." Ron said, "No, you can *feel* the road!" Same thing—different perspective. Positive versus negative. I had a decision to make. It was time to quit living in a negative world.

I prayed and told God that I wanted to trade in my old negative attitude for a positive one. I wanted to learn to see the good in every situation, to be a builder of people, not a destroyer. That day in the coffee shop, my sister set an example for me that forever changed my perspective.

Do not let any unwholesome talk come out of your mouths, but only what is helpful for building others up according to their needs, that it may benefit those who listen.

EPHESIANS 4:29

The Color of Sunshine

– Carol Kent –

A sister hears your heart before a word is spoken.
A sister tastes your tears and feels your joy.

Deborah Lindsay O'Toole

It had been the worst experience of my life. My boat had been rocked. My confidence had eroded. I questioned my worth as a mother, wife, sister, and friend. If I could have curled up in the embryo position, fallen asleep, and said goodbye to life, that would have been my choice. No, I wasn't actually suicidal—I just didn't think there was much about life that made it worth living.

My husband and I had received the devastating news that our son, a graduate of the U.S. Naval Academy, had been arrested for a heinous crime. The details surrounding this bizarre and shocking announcement took my breath away and put me into a deep depression. (I've told the full story in my book *When I Lay My Isaac Down*.)

Most of us have had a phone call, a diagnosis from a doctor, a financial reversal, a betrayal by a loved one, or a crisis in life that made us question God's love for us, our value to others, and our ability to go on with a normal life. This was me. I felt like standing up and saying, "I quit life! It's too hard! It's too unfair! I don't have the energy to fight anymore! I'm disappointed in God! I give up!"

In the middle of my depression and despair, the doorbell rang. It was a deliveryman with a large, covered object in his hand. With a cheery smile, he said, "Are you Carol Kent?"

I nodded.

"Well, it's your lucky day! Somebody must want to make you feel special today, and I have the privilege of delivering this gift. Enjoy your day!"

He disappeared as quickly as he came, and I found myself holding the covered object in my hands. It was enveloped in green florist paper. I took it to the island in the middle of my kitchen. As I tore away the protective covering, my eyes fell on one dozen of the most perfect yellow roses I had ever laid eyes on. I carefully opened the sealed envelope, and the note took me by surprise. It was from two of my sisters. This is what it read:

> Dear Carol,
> You once gave us some decorating advice that was very helpful. You said, "Yellow flowers will brighten any room." We thought you could use a little yellow in your life right now.
>
> Love,
> Bonnie & Joy

At that moment the skylight over my kitchen island revealed glorious sunshine pouring its rays on my beautiful bouquet. The yellow roses glistened in between the baby's breath and soft green fern, bringing an artistic glow to the unexpected gift.

Tears flooded my eyes, and I heard myself wailing like a mother mourning a great loss. I hadn't realized that, until this moment, I hadn't given myself permission to grieve over my deep disappointment or to express my feelings out loud. I had been slapping on a fake smile, being strong for others, and masking my heavy heart. It was a moment of honest grief and, for the first time in a long time, I felt like my life had a new degree of authenticity.

From that day on, yellow was my color of hope. My sisters sent yellow cards, yellow candles, and yellow packages. And they spread the word. Friends and other family members picked up on using the color of sunshine—yellow—to remind me that no matter what happens to us, no matter who disappoints us, no matter what crisis crosses our path, we can always find hope.

Friends, when life gets really difficult, don't jump to the conclusion that God isn't on the job. Instead, be glad that you are in the very thick of what Christ experienced. This is a spiritual refining process, with glory just around the corner.

1 PETER 4:12–13 MSG

Hospital Hair Care

– Linda Neff –

Sweet is the voice of a sister in the season of sorrow.

Benjamin Disraeli, from *Miriam Alroy*

"Would you like me to wash your hair for you?" I asked my sister caringly.

After a car accident left her confined to bed for three days, Margie looked forward to a chance for some personal grooming. She also marveled that so many people were bringing food to her family and taking care of other details while she was in the hospital. Flowers filled her room. This was not surprising to me at all.

"Relax, Margie. You've been helping friends, relatives, and neighbors for years. Now we're all delighted to have this opportunity to do something for you."

My sister is the kind of sibling and friend that everyone should have. If there is a need, she is there with a cleaning bucket, a paintbrush, and a plate of homemade dinner rolls. A church secretary for many years, Margie kept several ministers organized and free to use their own gifts and talents. Her husband and sons depended on her keyboard skills to complete most of their university essays. And many good relationships have been started and sustained around her beautifully set table of delicious food.

"I'll be back with the shampoo," I told her as I left to get my travel bag at our mother's house.

Back at the hospital, I carefully wet Margie's hair with warm water as she lay in bed, then I poured shampoo from the plastic bottle. "You have quite a buildup of grease and dirt, so I'm going to wash your hair twice. I didn't get much lather this time." There wasn't a whole lot of lather the second time either.

"Don't worry about it," Margie said graciously. "It feels so good to have it clean again."

We chatted some more. I glanced over at the side table where I had made a stand-up card. The verse on the card was significant to me: "You gave me skin and flesh and knit together bones and sinews. You ... were so kind and loving to me, and I was preserved by your care" (Job 10:11–12 TLB). We were all grateful to God for keeping Margie alive.

With a promise to visit the next day, I packed my shampoo bottle in a bag. Later, looking through the bag's contents, I discovered what I had used to wash my sister's hair—face cleanser. No wonder there weren't many bubbles!

We both laughed out loud at my mistake. And my sister recovered from her injuries in spite of my feeble attempt to help her—or perhaps her recovery was partly *because* of my silly mistake. Laughter *is* good medicine! Bonding with someone does not require perfection—just generous doses of being there and doing what we can. And laughing, especially about what doesn't turn out "just right."

My dear children, let's not just talk about love; let's practice real love. This is the only way we'll know we're living truly, living in God's reality. It's also the way to shut down debilitating self-criticism, even when there is something to it. For God is greater than our worried hearts and knows more about us than we do ourselves.

1 JOHN 3:18–20 MSG

Bicycles and Butterflies

– Bonnie Afman Emmorey –

Prayer is talking with God ... conversing with God about all the things that are important in life, both large and small, and being assured that He is listening.

C. Neil Strait

Summer in northern Michigan is an awe-inspiring experience. In our town of Gaylord, people say we have nine months of winter and three months of company—and that's not too far from the truth. Our winters last forever, but when summer finally arrives, we forget the weather we endured to get to this grand time of year.

We plan our yearly trip to Mackinac Island to include guests because it's fun to share the experience. The island is historically important, and it's well known for being the setting for the much-loved romantic movie *Somewhere in Time* starring Christopher Reeve and Jane Seymour, but that's not what draws me back. It's one of the most beautiful islands I have ever seen, complete with exquisite Victorian homes and turn-of-the-century charm. The famed Grand Hotel, sporting the world's longest front porch, at 660 feet, has rocking chairs overlooking the statuesque five-mile-long Mackinac Bridge, which connects the upper and lower peninsulas of Michigan. The island is famous for homemade fudge that melts in your mouth. Trips around the island reveal remarkable rock formations. The ferry ride to the island is always a treat, but the thing I like best is this—no motorized vehicles are allowed on the island. Visitors have to ride a bike or a horse to get anywhere. Since I am a non-athlete, I always rent a tandem bike with my husband. Then I can sit in the back and enjoy the ride.

The year my sister Carol, her husband Gene, and their two granddaughters, Chelsea and Hannah, joined us for our annual trek, my pattern was disrupted. The girls were at that in-between stage, ages six and nine—not quite ready to bike eight miles on their own but too old for child-size bike seats. The bicycle rental shops offered a creative alternative called tag-a-longs. This invention allows a small bicycle to be attached to a full-size bike and act almost like a tandem. The child on the small bike can help with pedaling or sit back and enjoy the ride. Our husbands attached tag-a-longs to both of their bikes, so that left Carol and me to fend for ourselves. We decided to rent the bicycle-built-for-two. What fun! It would be a sister experience to remember.

Less than ten minutes into our adventure we turned the tandem around and walked back to the bicycle shop. Completely unable to balance the bike, we were a threat to ourselves and everyone in our path. Carol and I laughed about being such klutzes but were unwilling to risk life and limb for the tandem sister ride.

After renting two single-seat bikes, we embarked on the scenic eight-mile trail around the island. It was on this trip that I saw a new side of my sister Carol. Our husbands, with Chelsea and Hannah on the tag-a-longs, were soon far ahead of us. Carol and I leisurely pedaled and talked as we rode. To my amazement, as we biked and chatted, Carol would suddenly start praying out loud, including God in our conversation as if He were riding right along with us. I had never seen or experienced that level of "praying without ceasing" before.

Carol and Gene's son, Jason, was incarcerated and awaiting trial for a serious crime; this situation was heavy on her heart. As we passed couples walking hand in hand along the path, I heard Carol pray, "Lord, in the middle of these devastating circumstances that have caused physical separation in a new marriage, please give Jason and his wife creativity as they learn to enjoy communicating with each other in new and creative ways."

As we saw birds fly by I heard Carol, "Father, would you allow my son to one day experience this same freedom?"

When we stopped at the butterfly house and spent an hour sitting and enjoying the remarkable experience of being in a room filled with different types of butterflies, Carol continued to pray for Jason. She conversed with God as easily as she did with me.

As I looked around at the spectacular color and variety of butterflies, I was reminded that they, too, were in captivity. Their freedom was limited to the walls around them, yet they brought great enjoyment to all who entered. Again I heard Carol's voice in prayer, "Dear God, I ask you to give Jason purposeful living within the confines of the jailhouse walls. Please provide an opportunity for meaningful conversation with a fellow inmate that will enable him to share his faith. Help him to see beauty in the day he is facing."

That trip to Mackinac Island was unlike any I have ever experienced. I came away a different person as I watched my sister share her heart with God. From the freedom of the bicycle ride to the confines of the butterfly house, her spirit communed with God without ceasing, and my understanding of walking and talking with God reached a new level.

My complaints about long winters now seem trite and petty. What a waste of energy! Yes, we are probably facing another long winter, but my heart is filled with memories of bicycles and butterflies, and of a sister who knows the true meaning of walking with God and praying without ceasing.

Be cheerful no matter what; pray all the time;
thank God no matter what happens. This is the way
God wants you who belong to Christ Jesus to live.

1 THESSALONIANS 5:16–18 MSG

Celebrating Our Differences

– Lisa Meiners –

Be yourself; everyone else is already taken.

Unknown

Compared to my sister, Laura, I'm a terrible cook. In my earlier years, I was tempted to think like this:

I can never live up to her standard of excellence in the kitchen. She can create gourmet meals out of leftovers. Her ability to please the family makes her everybody's favorite. My dinner table will never look as appealing as my sister's. I'm a book person; she's a food person.

Laura's skill in the kitchen is her greatest strength. Her strong point used to make me cower, but now I am her greatest champion.

She learned to care for others through cooking when our mom went back to school to get her master's degree. Laura would prepare meals while keeping an eye on my brother and me. And we would allow her to do this without offering to help in the kitchen so we could lie on our family room floor and watch TV together.

This is how her kitchen expertise began—and Laura's

culinary skills have only grown stronger with each passing year. Our family benefits from my sister's ability to work the kitchen like a pro. She hums a tune, licks her fingers, and laughs while hard at work. She makes difficult things look fun.

There was a time when I wanted to be like Laura, to shine like her. I wanted to receive accolades for creating something delicious with a little of *this* and a little of *that*. I thought, *If only I could create meals like she does—without a recipe card on the counter or propped up on the windowsill!*

But that's not me. I can hum a tune and lick my fingers with the best of them, but very few delicious meals are being produced in my kitchen. I have mastered a few. In any recipe, if there are six ingredients or less—I'm all in. If there are any more, I get lost in the grocery shopping before I even begin cooking.

My sister is great at what makes her heart sing. And I am equally strong at what makes *my* heart sing, which is quietly sitting and reading one book after another. I am never without a book when the moment arrives for this delightful activity. We have learned to appreciate one another for our differences and champion those differences. I delight in the delicious meals she prepares that I get to enjoy, and she relishes in my book summaries, thankful she doesn't have to read the book herself.

Laura relates to people by wowing them with a new, flavorful salad she whipped up with a few ingredients from her refrigerator, and I relate to people by wowing them with a lively conversation about the book series I just finished that I'm totally convinced everyone should read.

We are passionate about our individual delights, but we've learned a few lessons along the way. When it comes to growing in our relationship as sisters, we need to do these things:

- celebrate our differences
- avoid comparing skills, achievements, and proficiencies
- verbalize our appreciation for our sister's best talents
- delight in applauding each other's accomplishments in front of others
- thank God for making each of us unique

Being sisters is a gift I treasure. Since Dad and Mom have gone home to heaven, my connection with my sister, who couldn't be more different than me, is of utmost importance. We grow stronger in our relationship every year by living out the celebration of our differences.

Accept one another, then, just as Christ accepted you, in order to bring praise to God.

ROMANS 15:7

Sister Saves the Family Farm

– Nancy Hanna –

Elegant splendor reawakens our spirit's aching need for the infinite, a hunger for more than matter can provide.

Thomas Dubay, from *The Evidential Power of Beauty*

We call my sister Ginna "the Forrest Gump of the family." Who can forget the classic image of Tom Hanks playing the role of Forrest, who, through no intentions of his own, became the center of history's most important moments? To Ginna's way of thinking, that's the part she plays in our lives—the central character in the most pivotal moments of our family history. So in hindsight, it was obvious that my sister would be the one to save the family farm.

Since my earliest memories, my grandparents' farm was the perfect haven for the six of us ruffian siblings during our growing-up years. My brothers baled hay from the meadow, and we sisters learned to cut corn on the cob and snap beans fresh from the garden on Grandma's back porch, in preparation for freezing those vegetables for future dinners.

Grandma Alliene died very unexpectedly from a brain aneurysm during my sophomore year in college. She was gone from us in a matter of hours. The farm was quieter after that. Once the female nurturer was no longer there as our "emotional interpreter," we began to know Grandpa Edgar better. But years later when Grandpa died, the question arose—what would become of our much-loved farm?

It didn't take long for Ginna and her husband, Chris, to step up to the plate and establish the farm as our summer holiday gathering place for family reunions. And the farm got "glammed up" too. My creative sister had the house and outbuildings painted in the country French-inspired colors of butter cream and sea grass green, with a splash of the orange sprinkled in that matched some of the bell-shaped flowers in the nearby field. Ginna frequented farm auctions, and it didn't take long for newly caned chairs to surround Grandma's antique cherry dining room table. The plumbing was still slow and occasionally the well ran dry, but we gladly exchanged these minor inconveniences for the privilege of setting our feet in country grass and for the freedom of running outside in a summer rainstorm in our undies.

Then Ginna masterminded a start-up business on the property. After careful research, she discovered that growing organic lavender was a high cash crop—so she got to work. Or, I should say, our inventive sister put *all* of us to work—watering, cutting, bundling up the stems and hanging them to dry in the carriage house, buying ribbon, designing products, taking pictures, and designing a website. It took the sweat of faithful husbands, sisters, brothers, a supportive mother, nieces and nephews, along with additional girls and boys from the neighborhood. Sister Ginna dreamed it—and we came.

Yes, Ginna saved the farm. And every Fourth of July you can still find our clan gathering, goofing off, and connecting with each other on the property once owned by our grandparents—sparklers and rockets in hand. We play a mean game of croquet. The sisters can dance up a storm and cook up strawberry preserves at the same time. Ginna is at the helm of our purposeful antics, and we are her worker bees.

At Christmastime I bring magnolia leaves from Virginia to the Pennsylvania farm. Martha hits the Pittsburgh food-strip section for favorite cheeses and gourmet bread. Ginna and Chris order smoked salmon and tins of English biscuits for our festive celebrations. But most importantly, in these FaceTiming, texting, emailing, high-tech, media-saturated times, Grandma Alliene and Grandpa Edgar's legacy lives on, and our family gathers to smell the clover, mixed with the scent of Pennsylvania's finest lavender.

When we arrive, Ginna tells us about her latest lavender order on the web: "Some lady from San Francisco ordered eighty lavender-filled pouches for her shoes."

We say, "Who knew?" And then just as quickly, we chant, "Go Forrest, go!"

Better is a dinner of vegetables where
love is than a fatted ox and hatred with it.
The way of the lazy is overgrown with thorns,
but the path of the upright is a level highway.

PROVERBS 15:17, 19 NRSV

Hand-Me-Downs

– Trina Titus Lozano –

Among the things you can give and still keep
are your word, a smile, and a grateful heart.

Zig Ziglar

She was an only child, and I had one little brother. In a way only God could do, He gave me a big sister. At fifteen, Janece had beautiful skin glimmering with a California sun-kissed tan, and I was in awe of her coolness. Her personality, humor, trendy haircut, and bell-bottoms signified everything I wanted to be when I became a teenager.

I spent every summer of my childhood visiting my grandparents in California and Janece, my mom's first cousin, was often there too. I pretended she was my older sister. She taught me to paint my nails—fingers and toes, a full mani-pedi. I was only ten, but when we were together, I felt like a teenager.

Janece would often say, "I *love* having you here—it's just like having a little sister." This made me feel very special. Her room was a dream to hang out in. We talked for hours about boys, school, our favorite TV shows, and sometimes

God too. We exchanged funny family stories, and I eyed her every move and copied everything she did. I loved watching her rearrange her room and organize her closet and drawers. Sometimes she'd fill up a bag with hand-me-downs for me to take home. Her trash was my treasure.

Janece married at eighteen, and five years later I married; she had her first baby, and five years later I had mine; she gave birth to her second child, and five years later I followed in her footsteps. I never intended to be a copycat, but in hindsight I see that our lives were synchronized.

When Janece faced trials in her marriage, finances, and the loss of a parent, our sisterhood was proven by her vulnerability. She emerged from the fire of each situation with a newfound beauty—far beyond that of a super-cool teenager. Her faith and commitment to Jesus transformed her into a mature woman of God, and I looked up to her more than ever.

My future challenges mimicked those of Janece. When I faced adultery, bankruptcy, loss of precious relationships, and the death of my mom, I had my big sister's support to stabilize me. I was not alone. She had walked this road before, five steps ahead of me. Because of her, I knew I could face my pain with strength and a smile. She honored her marriage vows; she was resilient; and like her, I would be too.

Although we don't live near each other, we frequently send text messages or communicate via FaceTime—and we have never missed our annual summer visit. And Janece *still* sends hand-me-down treasures. Each time I receive a box, I feel loved.

Recently she asked my grandma (her aunt Oleta), about a retro cookie jar that sat on Grandma's countertop for decades. "Do you know where that old cat-shaped cookie jar is—the one with the red bow on top?"

When Grandma asked me about it, I knew exactly where it was. My mom had recently passed away, and I had packed it away with her things. I immediately wrapped it up with way too much bubble wrap, took it to UPS, and sent it to Janece.

When it arrived, she immediately texted me a picture with a note, saying, "My daughter has already claimed this cookie jar for her future countertop."

It was now my turn to be the giver of a priceless hand-me-down. And *no one* is more deserving than my big sister.

"You should remember the words of the Lord Jesus: 'It is more blessed to give than to receive.'"

ACTS 20:35 NLT

A Cherished Treasure

– Shirley Carter Liechty –

Duty makes us do things well,
but love makes us do them beautifully.

Phillips Brooks

As I rode the bus to school that day, a lone tear stung my cheek, and I stared out the window in silence. My face was flushed, my heart pounded, and my mind went in many different directions. I was fearful of being ridiculed by classmates once they learned my secret. My best friend, Sarah, met me outside school. As our eyes met, she knew something was terribly wrong. I burst into tears and exploded with my announcement: "My mom is going to have *another* baby."

But my embarrassment over having my peers discover my parents still engaged in enlarging our family (which already numbered six) was short-lived. Sarah's enthusiasm about the coming baby was contagious, and she soon had several of my fellow students and a favorite teacher involved in planning a baby shower for my new sibling. It didn't take long for my concerns about what others thought to disappear. The excitement and attention made the prospects of becoming a big sister again enjoyable and fun.

My beautiful new sister was born in mid-March, and my mother surprised me by allowing me to choose her name. I called her Marcia Ellen. Two months later I celebrated my eighteenth birthday, and just two weeks after that I graduated from high school.

The summer went by quickly, and I began my first semester of college in northeastern Indiana. As a freshman at a strict, conservative school, I wasn't allowed to leave the campus for a return trip home until Thanksgiving weekend. Although I enjoyed classes, making friends, and adjusting to being on my own, I also missed my family. By November I was ready for a break and more than eager to get home and see my growing baby sister.

Being home again was wonderful! On this holiday weekend our family of seven, plus my grandmother, packed into our vintage Mercury for a one-day visit to Aunt Ruby and Uncle Red. Their country home was charming, and the expansive property was complete with a stream, woods, and a pond—and Aunt Ruby was an incredible cook!

After the first forty miles, Dad pulled into a gas station. Looking over his shoulder into the backseat, he noticed that almost everyone had fallen asleep. Immediately suspecting a leak in the exhaust system, he began evacuating the family from the vehicle. The fumes hadn't affected my father or the other front-seat passengers (Grandma and me) because along the way he had opened the driver's window vent. As the doors were flung open, my brother exited the car and fell, nearly striking his head on the cement near the gas pumps. Service station attendants telephoned for help.

I noticed my mother was dazed and appeared to be in shock. I pulled back the baby blanket and looked at Marcia. I was horrified when I saw my baby sister's face. She was blue-gray in color, very cool, motionless, and her eyes were rolled back in her head. I took her from my mother's arms and quickly asked God to help me. I immediately remembered one of my classmates presenting a report on an important life-saving technique. Rather than doing nothing, my instinctive response was to at least try this procedure. Laying Marcia down, I carefully placed my mouth over hers and began mouth-to-mouth resuscitation.

For the next few moments, time stood still. Then finally, Marcia took a breath and began to cry. Moments later the neighborhood fire department rescue unit arrived and checked all of us. After hearing what transpired, one of the officers said, "That baby's big sister no doubt saved her life!" The color had come back into Marcia Ellen's face, and I breathed a huge sigh of relief.

Dad checked the car thoroughly and discovered the exhaust pipe had become plugged with mud when the car was driven off the road into a ditch earlier in the week. Now certain it was safe, we all climbed back into the car and resumed our trip. My dad wept on and off for most of the rest of the day, reminding us how much he loved us and telling us just how *special* this Thanksgiving really was!

Thoughts swirled in my mind. I'd been horrified the previous year when Mom found out she was going to have a baby. But the very thing I thought was going to be a major embarrassment turned out to be one of my greatest joys—the birth of Marcia Ellen. I breathed deeply and sighed, realizing that I had not only been given the privilege of naming my baby sister—God had allowed me to save her life. Although we would always be separated by years, she had become a cherished treasure, and I knew that I loved her dearly.

Love never gives up. Love cares more for others than for self.... Isn't always "me first,"... Trusts God always, ... keeps going to the end.

1 CORINTHIANS 13:4–7 MSG

Going Home

– Shari Minke –

You keep your past by having sisters. As you get older, they're the only ones who don't get bored if you talk about your memories.

Deborah Moggach

Our hearts pounded as we walked up the driveway. It had been years since we'd been inside our childhood home. A warm smile greeted us at the back door. "Hi! You must be the ladies who called requesting to go through the house. Come on in."

My sister Pat and I didn't get all the way through the doorway before we shouted in unison, "Look! The milk chute!" On more than one occasion, I had squeezed through the narrow passage like a contortionist. I became the family hero when my skinny frame snaked its way into the house, releasing the jammed lock.

As we stepped into the kitchen, memories gushed like rain from a downspout. "Boy, did we wash a lot of dishes!"

"Ha!" I responded. "Didn't you always have to go to the bathroom when it was your turn to wash dishes?"

"No! *You're* the one who did that!" Laughter followed.

As we entered the tiny dining room, we paused. This was Pat's favorite room. One afternoon many years earlier, Mom stopped her work in the kitchen to answer Pat's questions about Jesus. Leading Pat to sit by the bay window, Mom asked, "Pat, would you like to ask Jesus into your life?"

"Yes," she quickly responded.

After a simple prayer Mom suggested, "Let's write this date in your Bible. That way if you ever doubt that you belong to Jesus, you can see the date you made this choice written in black and white."

As Pat and I moved into the living room, tears welled in my eyes. This was *my* special place. On a crisp February morning in 1962, Mom greeted me with, "Shari! Today history is going to be made! A man named John Glenn is going to be the first American astronaut to blast off in a rocket ship and fly all the way around the world. We'll be able to see it on TV in just a few minutes!"

I didn't care about the blastoff. There were questions troubling me. Disregarding my mother's desire to watch the exciting news, I began pelting her with questions: "Why did I hear you and Dad praying for Uncle Jim so much before he came this weekend?"

"Because we want him to have a personal relationship with Jesus."

"What does that mean?" My five-year-old inquiring mind wanted to know.

Mom turned her back on the television. "Shari, the Bible says that all people have sinned. Sin is when you do something unkind, say something unkind, or even *think* something unkind. Sin separates us from God. God cannot be around sin. God loves us so much that He wants us to live with Him forever, but we can only live with God if we ask Him to forgive our sins and come to live in our hearts. You know how you get punished when you do something wrong?"

"Yes."

Mom stayed focused on my face. "The Bible says that God loves us so much that His Son, Jesus, came to earth and died on a cross to take all the punishment we deserve for being unkind. I do a lot of things for you. I cook your food. I wash your clothes. But there is one thing I can never do for you—I can't decide for you if you want Jesus to forgive your sins and be a part of your life."

"I *do* want to do that!" I declared.

Mom and I knelt beside each other. Even though I was very young, I knew there were times I'd been unkind to my brother and sisters, so I prayed, "Jesus, please forgive my sins and come into my heart." Mom prayed after me.

When we stood up, we had missed the rocket's exciting blastoff. Without any indication of disappointment, Mom hugged me. "Shari, today you went a whole lot farther than John Glenn!"

As my sister and I reminisced, the current homeowner

listened graciously. With tenderness in her eyes, she said, "I want the two of you to take your time and go through the whole house. Enjoy your memories."

We ascended the stairs to our former bedroom. Suddenly we felt like we were stepping back in time. Our bedroom was *exactly* as it had been twenty-some years earlier! We hugged each other and cried. This was the room where we had shared many secrets, dreams, and prayers.

Holding hands, we prayed one last time under the roof of our childhood home. We thanked God for a mom who didn't miss the moments when her daughters were ready to make the most important decision of their lives. Our hearts were joined in gratitude for a mom who stopped her work in the kitchen and stopped watching the television so that two little girls would not just be sisters on earth—but sisters for eternity!

Daughters, come and listen and let me teach you the importance of trusting and fearing the Lord.

PSALM 34:11 TLB

About Carol Kent

Carol Kent is a best-selling author and international speaker. With vulnerable openness, irrepressible hope, restored joy, and a sense of humor, she directs you to choices based on God's truth. Carol says, "When God writes your story, you will be in for the adventure of a lifetime!"

Carol is executive director of the Speak Up Conference, a ministry committed to helping Christians develop their speaking and writing skills. She and her husband, Gene, founded the nonprofit organization Speak Up for Hope, which benefits inmates and their families.

She holds a master's degree in communication arts and a bachelor's degree in speech education. She is a former radio show cohost and has often been a guest on Focus on the Family and many other media outlets.

Carol has trained Christian speakers for over twenty-five years. She has been a featured speaker at Women of Faith, Extraordinary Women, and Women of Joy arena events. She is the author of over twenty-five books, including the best-selling *When I Lay My Isaac Down* and *Becoming a Woman of Influence* (NavPress), a 365 page-per-day devotional titled *He Walks with Me* (Christian Art Gifts), the 2021 Christian Market Christian Living Book of the Year, *Staying Power: Building a Stronger Marriage When Life Sends Its Worst* (Revell, coauthored with Gene Kent and Cindy and David Lambert), and *Life Lessons for Moms* (Christian Art Gifts).

She and Gene are both fans of tracking down the best cup of coffee in every city they visit. Their favorite activity is watching sunsets together.

Connect with Carol

www.facebook.com/AuthorCarolKent
www.X.com/CarolKentSpeaks
www.instagram.com/CarolKentSpeaks
www.CarolKent.org
www.SpeakUpMinistries.com
www.SpeakUpConference.com
www.SpeakUpforHope.org
For information, call 586.481.7661

Contributors

Traci Ausborn has authored several nonfiction articles and is working on a Christian mystery novel series. A former church business manager and pastoral secretary, she enjoys speaking at conferences and facilitating training sessions at the corporate level. She serves as a program manager for Providence Health & Services and makes her home in Camas, Washington. She enjoys spending time with her husband, son, daughter-in-law, three grandchildren, as well as her dog, Bandit.

Dawn Baker, LMSW is the director for pregnancy counseling and infant adoption at Bethany Christian Services in Michigan. She has spoken around the country on university campuses with Students for Life groups, sharing about adoption and life-affirming choices. Dawn holds a master's degree in social work from Eastern Michigan University. She is a wife, mother, and nana and enjoys music ministry and women's ministry in her local church.

Barbara Bond-Howard worked for four decades as a recreational therapist and shares her expertise in continuing education. She counts a loving husband, three headstrong kids, four feisty grandkittens, two neurotic grandpups, a lovely garden, no shortage of Wisconsin cheese, a daunting Duolingo Spanish streak, and thousands of arboreal walks in the bouquet of her blessings.

Joy Carlson is a pastor's wife and teacher who wants to know Jesus the way He longs to be known and encourage others to know Him. As the mother of seven children and grandmother of thirteen, her experience with family and ministry has given her a passion for encouraging women in matters of faith, marriage, and parenting. Joy can be reached at: imjoybells@gmail.com.

Pam Cronk taught elementary school for twenty-six years. She enjoys traveling with her husband and spending time with her sisters. Pam has been involved in crafts of all sorts and enjoys working in her flower gardens as well as serving in her church.

Anne Denmark is a seasoned professional coach. She affirms the gifts in others and supports them in loving like Jesus. She has served as an instructor for Professional Christian Coaching Institute and as a faculty member of the Speak Up Conference with Carol Kent Ministries. Anne lives in Nashville, Tennessee with her husband, Don.

Jennie Afman Dimkoff is an author and international speaker for retreats, conferences, and for events on college campuses. She serves on the boards of Our Daily Bread Global Ministries and Speak Up for Hope. She is also on the faculty at the annual Speak Up Conference. Her website is www.JennieDimkoff.com.

Bonnie Afman Emmorey is the conference director for the Speak Up Conference, a ministry that equips Christian speakers and writers. She's also the director of Speak Up for Hope, a prison ministry. Bonnie and her husband, Ron, have two grown sons, two awesome daughters-in-law, and six delightful grands. They reside in Wichita, Kansas.

Brenda Fassett is first and foremost a believer in Jesus Christ. Her family includes her husband, Doug, three grown children, and two grandchildren. Brenda and Doug are actively involved in their local church in several leadership roles. Her days are filled with family, ministry, and enjoying retirement.

Jill Lynnele Gregory lives in the metro-Detroit area. She has four adult children. She and her husband continue to care for their special-needs adult daughter. Jill writes a blog, www.prayingforsarahg.com, to share what the Lord is teaching her on this autism journey. She can be contacted at gregoryfam1994@gmail.com.

Nancy Hanna is an NFP consultant on branding and storytelling. Her love of writing has included playwriting, TV show scripting and producing, and creative writing projects. Achievements include an Emmy Award as producer of *Aspiring Women,* Eugene O'Neill Playwriting finalist, and short plays published through Dramatic Publishing. Contact Nancy at nanhan3@gmail.com.

Jolanta Hoffmann is Choral Director at Chickahominy Middle School in Hanover County, Virginia. She teaches piano, voice, and guitar lessons, directing the children's choir and youth praise band at her church. She resides with her husband, Brad, and they enjoy frequent visits from her five grandchildren.

Toni Schirico Horras is a retired social worker and now a stay-at-home Grammie—a much better gig. Volunteer work for Safe Families for Children (www.safe-families .org) and quality time with girlfriends are top priorities. She makes her home in Des Moines, Iowa, but makes frequent trips to Chicago for blues and jazz fests. Email: toni.s.horras@gmail.com.

Page Hughes is the cofounder of Anchor Deep Ministries. She is the author of *Party with a Purpose*. Page enjoys speaking and writing, but her favorite jobs are pastor's wife and grandmother. Page's southern charm makes her a favorite speaker for women's events. For more information, visit her website at www.pagehughes.com.

Kelly King serves as women's minister at Quail Springs Baptist Church in Oklahoma City. She previously served as the manager of magazines/devotional publishing and women's ministry training for Lifeway Christian Resources. She is the author of *Ministry to Women: The Essential Guide to Leading Women in the Local Church*. She is a contributor to the *Lifeway Women's Bible*, as well as several Lifeway Women studies, numerous blogs, and articles. In addition, she was the cohost of the *MARKED* podcast for Lifeway Women. She has a master of theology degree from Gateway Seminary as well as a doctorate in ministry degree.

Pat Layton is an author, speaker, and coach with a passion for inspiring women on the "Quest of Faith." Pat and her husband have been married for over forty-five years and enjoy a growing family of twelve. You can find her planting flowers and fresh ideas in her she-shed in the mountains of North Georgia. Find her at www.patlayton.net.

Shirley Carter Liechty served as the administrative assistant for speaker and author Carol Kent for fifteen years. More recently, she joined her husband in retirement from pastoral ministry. She enjoys gardening, birdwatching, and photographing her grandchildren.

Trina Titus Lozano is a wife, mother of four, and grandmother of twelve. She is a licensed minister, pastoral counselor, and the coauthor of *Home Experience*. It has been said about Trina, "When she enters a room, she fills it with joy. Trina turns the ordinary into a party." Visit her website at www.homeexperience.global.

Lucinda Secrest McDowell was passionate about helping people choose lives of serenity and strength. A seasoned mentor, she was the award-winning author of sixteen books, including *Soul Strong* and *Life-Giving Choices.* She's at home with her Lord now, but she loved to encourage young mamas, coach writers and speakers, and speak blessing over hungry souls.

Lisa Meiners, founder of Deeper Still Ministries, is a Christian speaker, author, and Bible teacher. She grew up in Lima, Ohio, studied elementary education in Nyack, New York, and now delights in sitting on her back patio in Beavercreek, Ohio, soaking up the warm sun with a good book or conversation. She cherishes time with her husband, daughter, son-in-law, and two sons.

Dr. Nancy Meyer is an author, speaker, and courage coach who captivates audiences with her dynamic personality and her overcomer spirit. She is a wife, mom, proud grandma, and successful businesswoman, who was fifty-three when she signed up for her first Ironman triathlon, even though she had to learn to swim. Her best-selling book, *Defying Fear: Finding the Courage to Embrace Your True Value,* is available at DrNancyMeyer.com.

Shari Minke believes that with God *all* things are possible! He has transformed her from a shy, fear-filled person to a faith-filled speaker. Shari has a passion for encouraging others into a deeper walk with Jesus Christ. She and her husband, Tom, have four children and nine grandchildren.

Elizabeth Murphy is a popular conference and retreat speaker. Elizabeth delivers biblical truth with grace and humor from a deep well of compassion. She is a mother, grandmother, and a recent widow after forty wonderful years of marriage. She believes life is full, fun, and difficult all at once. To schedule Elizabeth as a speaker for your next event, go to elizabethmurphyspeaks.com.

Linda Neff is a writer, poet, and retired teacher. She and her husband live in the woods outside Orillia, Ontario, Canada. They have four grown children and six grandchildren. Linda can be contacted at lindamaryneff@gmail.com or through her blog at www.lindaneff.ca.

Cynthia Reynolds is a writer, artist, and spiritual director. She has a thriving art practice and frequently leads prayer and writing retreats. She and her husband live in Madison, Wisconsin and visit their three grandchildren in Boston as often as they can. Contact her at wildberrymom@gmail.com.

Allison L. Shaw was a project specialist for ProjectAttain!, a collective impact nonprofit that helped adults complete their education. She is passionate about curriculum development, post-secondary education, and great books. Allison, Michael, and their three children are based in Nashville, Tennessee.

Cynthia Spell is a Christian counselor, keynote speaker, and the author of *Deceived by Shame, Desired by God.* Her heart's desire is to teach women this truth: there is nothing you've done that is beyond God's redemption. He can turn our brokenness into a beautiful mosaic masterpiece.

Learn More About Carol & Gene Kent's Nonprofit Organization, SpeakUpforHope.org

We seek to help individuals and ministry leaders find ways to support and positively impact their local jail and prison ministries.

ENCOURAGE

- Provide resources needed by inmates including electronic equipment, educational materials, large print Bibles, books, greeting cards and sports equipment.
- Provide resources needed for visitation areas including games, cards, coloring books, and crayons for use by prisoners and their families.
- Offer resources by Carol Kent.
- Provide information on Boxes of Hope for the moms and wives of inmates.

EDUCATE

- Assist churches or individuals with information on working with prison chaplains, program directors, and wardens.
- Provide information on materials available that will teach inmates important life skills, such as practical money management, communication skills, positive marriage and parenting techniques.
- Provide teaching programs and Bible study workbooks for inmate-facilitated classes.

EQUIP

- Provide communications training for people doing evangelism and Bible teaching.

For more information, go to https://speakupforhope.org/

Learn More About Carol's Training for Christian Speakers and Writers

Be a part of the next generation of skilled Christian communicators. Hone your craft with like-minded believers with Carol and her team of gifted faculty members at the annual Speak Up Conference.

This three-day equipping conference is held annually in Grand Rapids, Michigan, or join us virtually from anywhere in the world.

You can select either the Writing Track or the Speaking Track

- ⊘ Learn how to craft a book proposal
- ⊘ Meet with top literary agents, publishers, editors, or speaking coaches (live conference only).
- ⊘ Gain the tools needed to move forward in an ever-changing industry.
- ⊘ Discover the latest trends from industry leaders.
- ⊘ Grow your platform through social media, email, and online networking.
- ⊘ Network with other Christians who are passionate about speaking and writing for God's glory.

For information, go to https://speakupconference.com/